REAL
NEAR DEATH EXPERIENCE
STORIES

REAL

NEAR DEATH EXPERIENCE

STORIES

*True Accounts of Those Who Died
and Experienced Immortality*

RANDY KAY & SHAUN TABATT

© Copyright 2022–Randy Kay and Shaun Tabatt

All rights reserved. This book is protected by the copyright laws of the United States of America. This book may not be copied or reprinted for commercial gain or profit. The use of short quotations or occasional page copying for personal or group study is permitted and encouraged. Permission will be granted upon request. Unless otherwise identified, Scripture quotations are taken from The Holy Bible, English Standard Version® (ESV®), copyright © 2001 by Crossway, a publishing ministry of Good News Publishers. Used by permission. All rights reserved. Scripture quotations marked NIV are taken from the HOLY BIBLE, NEW INTERNATIONAL VERSION®, Copyright © 1973, 1978, 1984, 2011 International Bible Society. Used by permission of Zondervan. All rights reserved. Please note that Destiny Image's publishing style capitalizes certain pronouns in Scripture that refer to the Father, Son, and Holy Spirit, and may differ from some publishers' styles. Take note that the name satan and related names are not capitalized. We choose not to acknowledge him, even to the point of violating grammatical rules.

DESTINY IMAGE® PUBLISHERS, INC.
P.O. Box 310, Shippensburg, PA 17257-0310
"Promoting Inspired Lives."

This book and all other Destiny Image and Destiny Image Fiction books are available at Christian bookstores and distributors worldwide.

For more information on foreign distributors, call 717-532-3040.
Reach us on the Internet: www.destinyimage.com.

ISBN 13 TP: 978-0-7684-6405-4
ISBN 13 eBook: 978-0-7684-6406-1

For Worldwide Distribution.
1 2 3 4 5 6 7 8 / 26 25 24 23 22

CONTENTS

Foreword		7
Introduction		11
Chapter 1	What Is a Near-Death Experience?	19
Chapter 2	Jim Woodford Died and Spent 11 Hours in Heaven	25
Chapter 3	Lung Transplant Recipient Mike Olsen Died and Met His Organ Donor in Heaven	63
Chapter 4	Ivan Tuttle Died and Encountered Satan in Hell Before Seeing God in Heaven	93
Chapter 5	Captain Dale Black Died in a Plane Crash, Find Out What He Saw in Heaven	139
Afterword: What Do These Near-Death Experience Stories Mean for Me?		179

FOREWORD

I am absolutely delighted to be asked by Shaun Tabatt and Randy Kay to write a foreword to their collection of vignettes regarding near-death experiences. Having knowledge of my own NDE as described in my book, *Heaven, An Unexpected Journey*, I feel uniquely qualified to speak with clarity on what I consider to be a profound turning point in my life and my personal journey to God.

Since mankind first gazed into the starlight of the night sky, the fascination and fear of what waits beyond dying and death has captivated the imagination of every civilization in history. This went far beyond the macabre and superstitions to a belief that an afterlife might exist in which lavish rewards or punishment awaited. The great culture of the Egyptians probably best exemplified this with the erection of massive temples and pyramids and the involved process of mummification to ease the journey of the dead to the underworld. The advent of the Abrahamic teachings of the Jewish people was the first glimmer of light of a God who existed and embodied the teachings of love, charity, and kindness if a strict moral code was adhered to. It also gave mankind the hope that the abode of the Creator was a place that all men and women could aspire to—the kingdom of Heaven.

I sincerely believe that in this present day God is using NDEs to make the reality of Heaven front and center right now. The world is in great peril and many believe it to be a sign of end times careening toward us. I also believe that the interconnected world we live in now has allowed numerous people who have had an out-of-body experience to bring it to the attention of the world through the extensive reach of the internet. That simply wasn't possible 20 years ago. I am constantly amazed at how my own NDE has reached millions of people all over the world and thousands of them tell me every week about how it has encouraged their own walk with Jesus. Many of them shyly tell me of their encounters with loved ones or Jesus during death incidences and that they were afraid to go public for fear of ridicule or being ostracized from friends and family. Near-death experiences are far more common than previously thought and will continue to grow in my opinion. I do not agree with those critics and cynics who refer to these wonderful events as "heavenly tourism." How lacking in faith and belief! Of course, there are people who try to gain attention or attempt to monetize false events and they will always be with us, but a day of reckoning awaits them!

In my own situation, I never dreamed of the chain of contacts and opportunities that came my way to help get my story known. From the wonderful folks at Destiny Image Publishers and Nori Media Group to appearances on Sid Roth's *It's Supernatural!*, on CBN's *The 700 Club*, and hundreds of churches that opened their doors to me, I owe them all a huge thank you. And of course, my greatest thanks go to Jesus, whose divine guidance I see in everything my wife Lorraine and I do for Him.

FOREWORD

Most recently, Shaun Tabatt and Randy Kay invited me on their 2 Christian Dudes podcast and as of a few weeks ago over 2.5 million people had viewed the program! Their unique approach of seeing near-death experiences as both a supernatural and divine happening will encourage many to share the secrets of their hearts.

Your Constant Friend,
Jim Woodford
Bestselling Author of *Heaven, An Unexpected Journey*

INTRODUCTION

RANDY

Following my afterlife experience, I felt as though I was alone with my encounter. No one could possibly have had anything close to the grandeur and the closeness to Jesus that I had experienced, I thought. But after listening to many accounts of others who also experienced God in Heaven, I realized that I was not alone. Some survivors of death teared up in recollecting their encounter with Jesus, as did I. All were dramatically changed as a result of their afterlife event, like me. When Shaun Tabatt and I began interviewing these afterlife survivors, the veil between reality on earth and the hyperreality in Heaven lifted to expose the truth that Heaven is even more real than this world, and only those who had experienced this truth in the afterlife could fully understand this phenomenon.

The afterlife remains a mystery to those who have not yet crossed the great divide between this life and what comes next. Many desperately seek answers. Some have treated me and other afterlife survivors as though we possess some clairvoyant power when, in fact, we are sharing our own experiences that may or may not be identical to the one you will invariably experience. Some like me speak of a future with Jesus in Heaven. Some have told of us of their encounter in hell. Others have painted a surreal picture of the afterlife. The big question of what comes next may be answered through the pages of this book by first answering some other questions: What was the state of the person before and after they died and entered life thereafter? Were these survivors believers in Jesus Christ as their Lord and Savior prior to their clinical death? Were they living a moral life or were they indulging their selfish desires prior to their heart stopping? What was their belief or religion prior to their near-death experience? The answers to these questions can help ascertain what you can expect after you depart this life.

What I have noticed is that there are some common threads that weave together an otherworldly tapestry foretelling what you can expect in the life hereafter. You can find the answers to your future if you carefully seek the truth expressed in the stories you will hear. I encourage you to ask God's Holy Spirit to open your spiritual eyes to assimilate what God wants you to know, and for God to increase your spiritual understanding to synthesize all that you will note throughout the pages of this book so that you can fathom the Holy Spirit's insights about your eternity. What we noticed in the testimonies of believers in Jesus as their Lord and Savior is a shared sense of God's Love and a welcoming Presence that ushered them into a paradise replete with everlasting joy. Others testify of experiences, both good and bad, rather than of the personhood of Jesus in Heaven.

I noticed that those who knew Jesus before their death deeply encountered Jesus in Heaven, whereas those who were not

INTRODUCTION

believers or just acknowledged Jesus superficially realized a more distant God, or some other beings like angels, or for atheists, a hellish place. The spiritual state of the person just prior to his or her experience seemed to determine their intimacy with God as told in Romans 6:8: "Now if we died with Christ, we believe that we will also live with him" (NIV). This helps answer the question why near-death experiences vary and why some see the person of God, whereas others see some vague figure. Other factors also can determine personal encounters, such as what God wants to communicate with a person as well as the vastness of Heaven itself.

While continuing to question why experiences may vary, you might also ask this important question: Why is it important to know about Heaven and the afterlife? The Bible mentions Heaven over 500 times. In the Gospels, Jesus often describes and teaches about Heaven using parables such as the Mustard Seed (Matt. 13:31-32), the Hidden Treasure (Matt. 13:44), and the Pearl (Matt. 13:45-46). Heaven should be the aim for all believers so that our spirits can be reunited with God in Christ. Heaven exists in a realm where everything operates according to God's will.

We found that while most afterlife experiences might appear alluring, those experiences apart from the lordship of Jesus Christ reveal a different story. These experiences not rooted in the Christian faith are viewed through the perspective of universalism, a belief in the salvation of all souls. These accounts generally focus on the self, whereas Christian experiences focus on the Presence of God being imparted to those with whom the Spirit of Christ enjoys a relationship. The difference would be like describing a cosmic force rather than a familiar person. Christian afterlife experiences focus primarily on the person of Jesus, whereas non-Christian experiences tend to focus on an abstract consciousness.

We chose to include testimonies that honor Jesus Christ in this book because those accounts tend to lead toward very real discoveries, whereas the more ethereal and universalistic experiences tend to raise more questions than answers. In the case of the apostle Paul, the religious leaders in the city of Lystra (now part of present-day Turkey) ordered Paul's stoning and subsequently he was left for dead. As recorded in 2 Corinthians, Paul noted his experience in the "third heaven" 14 years after it occurred, presumably following his stoning. "Whether in the body or out of the body I do not know; God knows," states Paul. Today we would call this a near-death experience or an afterlife experience. Paul did not go into detail about his experience. In fact, he waited long after his experience to tell this story, and one can surmise that Paul did not want the description of Heaven to cloud his more important message of Jesus as the Messiah, the "anointed" one, and as the Immanuel, meaning "God is with us" as described in the Book of Isaiah (7:14). But everything Paul taught about God's truth came with the implicit understanding that Heaven lay in the future of the believer in Jesus as Lord and Savior.

Why did Paul not provide a detailed description of Heaven as many in this book do? Because, perhaps, God's Word had not yet been fully recorded in the Bible during the earthly life of Paul and therefore he felt it paramount to establish God's Word. Today the

INTRODUCTION

Gospel of Jesus Christ has reached the farthest ends of the earth and the prophecies foretelling Christ's return appear to have been fulfilled. Perhaps God is unveiling the mysteries of Heaven today in preparation for the final fulfillment of God's Word as described in the Book of Revelation. If you, like me, believe that we are living in the final chapter of all time, then it makes perfect sense that God is releasing the details of Heaven in preparation for our imminent return to Heaven—our real home.

Coincidentally, I did not feel released to publicly share my account of being in Heaven with Jesus until 14 years after my afterlife experience—the same number of years that passed before Paul released his account. I believe that God is preparing our hearts for eternity through the stories you are about to read. The analogy that comes to mind is when my father shared with me the secrets of living apart from my childhood home shortly before leaving for college. "I want you to be prepared for what's to come, Randy," he said. And then my father began to explain my "grown-up life" based on how he expected my life to proceed in my new world. I think God is telling us something similar by revealing the secrets of Heaven to us now. God wants you to know what you can expect after this "nanosecond" of life in this world passes into eternity. He also wants to quicken your wisdom to live your life now in accordance with the lessons that these experiences impart to us from Heaven. It is critically important to know about Heaven, because Heaven teaches us how to live today.

Many have contacted me wanting to know if they can be assured of being in Heaven on the day they depart from this world. I usually cite this passage from Romans 10:9-10: "If you declare with your mouth, 'Jesus is Lord,' and believe in your heart that God raised him from the dead, you will be saved. For it is with your heart that you believe and are justified, and it is with your mouth that you profess your faith and are saved" (NIV). Salvation does not give us license to sin and sin again; it establishes relationship with Jesus Christ. Once we begin our journey with Jesus, the goal in this life is to follow Him all the way to Heaven.

In Heaven, all I wanted to do was please Jesus. I just wanted to worship Him and to follow His directions. I wanted nothing else but to please my Lord, because all of me was what He wanted. As you read each account of the afterlife, ask yourself this single question: "What do I want to do differently today to honor God more fully?" Will you spend more time with God in prayer, study, and fellowship? Will you sacrifice something that is hindering your relationship with Christ? Will you thank God more often? Will you believe in God's truth instead of listening to the ways of this world?

These are some of the questions I hope you will ask yourself. My own account of Heaven was shared in tears while remembering God's unfathomable Love. Look for that Love, the person of Love, God (1 John 4:16), as you embrace these accounts into your heart. Cherish them with the sacredness from which they were created. Know that many of them were born from a stilled heart on what would have been the author's deathbed if not for the resurrection power of Jesus Christ. Believe them, because they are shared not with a desire for self-aggrandizement; rather,

INTRODUCTION

from humble attitudes of sacrifice because those who shared their stories often faced the ridicule of doubters after doing so.

In this book, Shaun and I present to you Heaven. We present to you your future in Christ—get ready for your next life. For those who are in Christ Jesus, the best is yet to come!

SHAUN

It was through working with Randy Kay on his book *Dying to Meet Jesus* that I first got interested in near-death experiences and heaven encounters. A few years later, I would have the privilege of partnering with Randy to release another book titled *Revelations from Heaven*.

In the months before the book hit the market, Randy and I launched a podcast called "2 Christian Dudes" in which we've interviewed many men and women who, like Randy, have had their own afterlife encounters, some of them experiencing both heaven and hell.

We couldn't have been more blown away by the response. We've received thousands of emails and comments about how people have encountered God through these conversations. People who are depressed and suicidal find hope. People who didn't know Jesus accept him as Lord and Savior after watching an interview.

This book, *Real Near Death Experience Stories*, shares four of the most impactful interviews we released in season one of the podcast. My prayer is that those of you who encounter the amazing testimonies in these pages will have the same sorts of God encounters reported by the men and women who watched and listened to the interviews. May heaven become as real and tangible to you as it is to the people whose stories you read in this book.

ONE

WHAT IS A NEAR-DEATH EXPERIENCE?

We're honored that you've decided to join us on a journey into four amazing true accounts of the afterlife. We realize that for some of you, this may be the very first time you're learning about near-death experiences, or NDEs as they're often called for short.

The Merriam-Webster Dictionary defines a near-death experience as "an occurrence in which a person comes very close to dying and has memories of a spiritual experience (such as meeting dead friends and family members or seeing a white light) during the time when death was near." This is a good working definition. However, it is worth noting that many of the people who report having a near-death experience were not only very close to death, but were verifiably clinically dead during their afterlife encounter. While both types of experiences are generally referred to as an NDE, in Randy's and my experience there does seem to be some variance in experience between those who were close to dying versus those who were clinically dead.

If you take some time to explore the wide array of testimonies and encounters that make up the near-death experience space, you'll soon discover that it is an extremely diverse field of study with many worldviews and faiths on display. This is important to keep in mind when you're reading or listening to an afterlife testimony, as the person's faith and worldview informs how they have processed their otherworldly experience and how they're sharing it with you. Randy and I approach this topic from a distinctly Christian worldview and seek to understand these conversations through the lens of the Bible and the teachings of orthodox Christianity.

Since I mentioned *worldview* and *Bible* in the previous paragraph, you may now be wondering if we can find any near-death experiences in the pages of Scripture. First let's look at what the apostle Paul says in 2 Corinthians 12:2-4.

> *I know a man in Christ who fourteen years ago was caught up to the third heaven—whether in the body or out of the body I do not know, God knows. And I know that this man was caught up into paradise—whether in the body or out of the body I do not know, God knows—and he heard things that cannot be told, which man may not utter.*

Second, let's look at the martyrdom of Stephen in Acts 7:54-60.

WHAT IS A NEAR-DEATH EXPERIENCE?

Now when they heard these things they were enraged, and they ground their teeth at him. But he, full of the Holy Spirit, gazed into heaven and saw the glory of God, and Jesus standing at the right hand of God. And he said, "Behold, I see the heavens opened, and the Son of Man standing at the right hand of God." But they cried out with a loud voice and stopped their ears and rushed together at him. Then they cast him out of the city and stoned him. And the witnesses laid down their garments at the feet of a young man named Saul. And as they were stoning Stephen, he called out, "Lord Jesus, receive my spirit." And falling to his knees he cried out with a loud voice, "Lord, do not hold this sin against them." And when he had said this, he fell asleep.

Scholarly opinions vary on whether we can look to these and other verses as true NDE accounts recorded in the Bible. However, from my vantage point, what is recounted in both of these passages fits within the range of the afterlife experiences Randy and I have encountered in our research and interviews. So, can we find near-death experiences in the Bible? My answer is yes. The afterlife encounters are there to be found if we have the eyes to see them.

One last thing we want to equip you with as we begin our journey into these amazing afterlife encounters is a list of things to watch for. As you become more familiar with NDEs, you'll start to see some common occurrences that show up in the majority of these accounts. Here are ten things to keep an eye out for:

- OBE/out-of-body experience: The experience of your spirit rising out of your body. You're often aware of the details of what is going on around your body, even though you are not in a conscious state.

- Tunnel: As a person's spirit is transitioning from the physical world to the spiritual world, people often recount seeing and being pulled into a tunnel.

- Bright light: There are many occurrences of bright lights during NDEs. They tend to be an indicator of coming into the proximity of God the Father, Jesus, and sometimes angels.

- Torment: Many people recount torment by demons and/or an awful experience in hell before transitioning into heaven.

- Cry for help: Many people recount crying out for help during the above-mentioned time of torment. This often results in either Jesus or angels showing up to rescue them and escort them into heaven.

- Life review: A review of the good and bad things that you did in life.

- Encountering friends or loved ones: People often report encountering deceased friends and family members in heaven.

- Encountering animals/pets: People often report encountering a beloved deceased pet in heaven.

WHAT IS A NEAR-DEATH EXPERIENCE?

- Saturated in love: Love permeates everything in heaven. Many people say they felt completely and totally immersed in love during their time in heaven.

- Communicating in heaven: You don't need to talk in heaven. Communication is instantaneous. The best way to describe it is spirit to spirit or thought to thought.

Now that you have an overall context for what you're going to encounter in these testimonies, let's begin the journey. Our prayer is that each conversation will stretch you, encourage you, and bring you closer to a full and complete realization that the resurrected Jesus is real and heaven is a real place He longs for you to call home someday.

TWO

JIM WOODFORD DIED AND SPENT 11 HOURS IN HEAVEN

MEET JIM WOODFORD

A successful airline pilot and businessman, Jim had it all—a loving family, substantial wealth, and all of the good things that come with it. But none of this was enough to satisfy the emptiness he felt in his heart. He always hungered for something more. And then he died.

Jim was never a religious man. When it came to matters of God and faith, he was ambivalent. But as he lay in the hospital bed, clinically dead for more than 11 hours, his consciousness was transported to the wonders of heaven and the horrors of hell. When he returned to this world, he brought back the missing peace his soul had been longing for.

Join Jim Woodford on this unforgettable journey into the afterlife!

INTERVIEW WITH JIM WOODFORD

RANDY: Jim Woodford was a successful businessman and pilot, as Shaun mentioned, and then a rare disease killed him and he had an experience with heaven. You're going to want to read it straight through because, at the end, you're going to encounter something very encouraging. So, Jim, please share your story. It is absolutely fascinating.

JIM: Well, thank you, Randy and Shaun, for having me and for the opportunity to give people hope. If you ever considered yourself a lost cause, I'm the walking billboard when it comes to God. So my book that I wrote, *Heaven: An Unexpected Journey*, truly was an unexpected journey. Randy, feel free to interrupt me because there's so much to tell you in such a short time that I always feel a little panicky because I feel if I leave something out, it may be the one thing that would bring someone closer to God. So please bear with me. So to give you a little background, this happened to me back on April 21, 2014. I was not a Christian. I was raised Catholic, but it didn't mean a whole lot to me except there was a good hockey team at the church.

I'm Canadian. I was born in Newfoundland, Canada, which is sort of in the north-northeast, where summer is on a Wednesday from 2:00 to 4:00, but I loved it and it was my home. My dad died when I was very young. I was only two and my mom was left a widow with two young boys and she was only 23. I had a wonderful upbringing. We lived with my paternal grandparents and they were a wonderful Irish Catholic family. And so nothing traumatic happened to me. I don't remember my father, of course, but we were surrounded by love in a remote area of the Canadian hinterlands. And I had a good life. One of the things that I got used to as a young boy was watching the seaplanes that would come in and land on the lakes to bring supplies and that sort of thing.

I became enamored with aviation. By the time I reached 18, that was what I wanted to do with my life. And although we were quite poor, my mom arranged somehow for me to borrow the funds to put me through aviation school. At 18, I graduated; it was back in 1967. Imagine a world without cell phones or satellites. And of course, growing up in the bush, I was able to land a job with a bush flying company. From there, my career eventually blossomed into flying larger aircraft and working all over the world.

Like anyone starting a new job, I loved it. If you're lucky enough in life to have a profession that you love so much, you'd do it for free, and on top of that they paid you ridiculously large amounts of money to do it, you're very fortunate. That was me and I loved it. I loved the travel and eventually did a lot of work out of England and into Africa and South America on special freight airlines. So I had a good career, but, you know, I look back now in the clear light of hindsight. I remember those endless hours on a night flight over, say, the South China Sea where it's so black, you can't even see where the sky ends and the earth begins, and I'd look up at the stars. And you would think that I would have thought more about God than I did.

SHAUN: You didn't think about God in those days?

JIM: No, but I was never agnostic. I think, like most people, I hoped that someone was in charge of the chaos, but I never sought it out. I continued to live a life that became quite successful, and I invested my money wisely at the beginning of the tech boom in the eighties. And I had a good life. My nickname, by the way, was Diamond Jim, because I seemed to have such good luck. I survived an engine failure at 35,000 feet; I had business deals that just blossomed—not out of any kind of particular intelligence on my part, just keeping my ear to the ground around smart people. That made me very comfortable in life, shall we say.

So life was good. I married. I met my wife on horseback, which I mention because horses play an important part in this story. Growing up as a child in a remote area, my grandfather logged with horses. I grew up crawling under the bellies of horses and watching my grandfather and learning from him. So I've always had a love for horses. As I'm sitting here talking to you, I'm looking out the window at my horses as we speak.

RANDY: Jim, I know horses have been a big part of your journey both here on earth and in heaven. I know I'm getting ahead in the story, but I can't wait for our audience to learn about the horses God had waiting for you in heaven.

JIM: I suppose like a lot of people, not just of my generation, but going back to the beginning of mankind, my main focus in life

I tell people that you know when you've done something catastrophic. And by catastrophic, I mean life-ending. Suddenly my lungs started to seize; it was as though the cab of the truck was filling with water and I kept raising my head to try to breathe and I could not. And that was the moment of realization that I was dying. And remember, I wasn't agnostic, but I believe the old saying, "There are no atheists in foxholes." There are no atheists dying in trucks either. I remember raising my hand—it was shaking violently—to the setting sun, and from somewhere really deep inside of me, a place that I had never been to, came this overwhelming feeling of "not fair, not fair." I'd had engine failures. I'd landed in difficult situations. It wasn't fair. It was a feeling of remorse that I had lived by a standard that many would have thought the ultimate success, and I'd never thanked the Creator, if He existed. And so I raised my shaking hands to the setting sun, and I cried out the first three of six words. And the first three words that I cried out were, "God, forgive me."

> ***The first three words that I cried out were, "God, forgive me."***

SHAUN: Jim, we've heard from so many of our near-death experiencer friends that they like you cried out to God in their final moments before they crossed to the other side. Tell us, what happened next?

was the achievement of wealth because wealth gave you freedom. So I thought, and I worked toward that, and I became good at it and was rewarded accordingly. But little did I realize how hollow that is. I enjoyed my collection of British sports cars, my large boat, a new airplane, but then I remember lying awake at night and thinking, "Is this all there is?" I interpreted that as meaning I needed more cars or a faster airplane or a bigger boat, so the next day I would go and buy them. But what I was searching for was something far beyond the wealth of this world. I just didn't know it. I look back now in absolute amazement that I never realized it was the absence of God in my life that was creating this emptiness.

So I had a charmed life; a beautiful, loving family; and wealth sufficient to take care of pretty much anything I wanted or needed. On top of that, I was blessed with good health all my life and never had more than a head cold. But in 2009 and 2010, I began to feel different. Of course, I put it to one side because my nickname was Diamond Jim—I could overcome anything.

I had a charmed life; a beautiful, loving family; and wealth sufficient to take care of pretty much anything I wanted or needed.

Arrogance is a difficult thing. You don't really realize how arrogant you are until you're faced with a true calamity in your life. I have learned the hard way that you have to come to the end of yourself before you find the beginning of God.

SHAUN: That's so true. Coming to terms with our own arrogance and pride is one of the most difficult, yet profound and important lessons for us to learn on our journey with God.

JIM: That's what happened to me. So to get to the point, I became more and more ill and then woke up one morning and was unable to stand. I was quite ill. It was a Sunday morning, and my wife had gone to church. Of course, I never went.

Because it was a Sunday, I had to wait until Monday to see my doctor. When I went to see him, he examined me and said, "Well, I think you just have maybe a flu that's coming on. So just go home and rest." I did, and nothing improved. In fact, it went downhill, and a couple days later I couldn't keep food down and the paralysis was becoming more pronounced. I was having difficulty walking. So I went in again, and now he was annoyed with me and assured me I was fine. The blood work had not come back yet, but just go home and rest. Two days later, I dragged myself in there again, and this time I collapsed in the parking lot. Now they were paying attention. My wife advocated very strongly that I be admitted to the hospital.

This was 2009, and I don't blame the physicians for this. No one could pinpoint what was wrong with me. At first, I thought

I had multiple sclerosis, but that proved not to be true. Actually what was happening was I had contracted a disease called Guillain-Barré syndrome. For those who may not be familiar with it, it was first isolated by Dr. Guillain and Dr. Barré of Paris right around World War I. Not a lot of people have it, although there's more transmission of it now with the Zika virus. Guillain-Barré, named after the two doctors, is the erosion of the myelin sheath on your brain stem. The nerves react by not being able to perform the functions that they were created for. The result is a lot of pain, tremendous pain, and nothing works.

So I was in the hospital and they couldn't figure out what was wrong with me. Many physicians never see this disease in their entire career, so they don't recognize it. I had one doctor tell me Guillain-Barré is a small footnote in their studies. They brought in a consulting neurologist who had had one Guillain-Barré patient in his lifetime. They did a test that required taking fluid from my spine, and they found very elevated protein levels and immediately diagnosed it as Guillain-Barré. Then they use plasmapheresis and auto-immunoglobulin therapy, but you have a window of opportunity to stop it. The paralysis creeps up, and if it gets into your lungs, you simply die.

By this time almost two weeks had passed and I was really in the throes of being quite ill. They started intensive blood transfusions to try and overcome it, yet slowly but surely it went into full-blown Guillain-Barré. At first, I started to get better, and you would have thought, with what I had faced, that I might have taken the time to cast my eyes heavenward and say, "God, I may not have believed, but thank You." Not me. Arrogance, as I said, is a terrible thing. And I say this with all respect—airline captains are somewhat guilty of arrogance. We don't naturally start that way. But when you spend your life delivering hundreds of thousands of people safely to their destination, you feel quite good about that. And you have to be careful because that sometimes becomes arrogance. Think about that for a moment. You're flying through severe weather, 30,000 to 35,000 feet, and sitting behind you are a couple of hundred people just wanting to get home to their family and they are your responsibility. And so you can come by arrogance naturally.

RANDY: Stewarding that many souls at 30,000–35,000 feet is indeed a responsibility to not take lightly.

JIM: I got through it. I went through a tremendous amount of physiotherapy, learned to walk again, learned how to swallow, learned how to speak, but was left with tremendous body pain all over. And I'm not talking inconvenient pain, Randy and Shaun, I'm talking pain that's all-consuming. And those of you who are going through or have had experience with that level of pain, you know it eclipses everything else in your life.

That level of pain eclipses everything else in your life.

When I got well enough to travel, I went to all the best medical treatments around the world to try to find some sort of cure or relief. As I said, relatively speaking there were so few cases of Guillain-Barré that there's been very little research into it. I tried standard medications and so on; they did not work. A specialist did recommend that I try an experimental drug from England, and my doctors got special permission from the Canadian health authorities to import the therapeutic drug on a temporary basis to see if it would help. And you know something? It did. It wasn't an immediate cure, but I could have at least three or four hours of the day when the pain had decreased by 75 percent, and that was a wonderful gift.

I also discovered that if I took more than the prescription called for, the pain relief was greater and it lasted longer. And here we enter the slippery slope of overmedicating oneself. But having spent three years in absolute pain and isolation, and having lost my ability to ride my horses, to fly a plane, to do all the sports that I loved, suddenly being able to get some semblance of that back—I grabbed at it. Unknown to my doctors and unknown to my wife, I began to take more of the drug. Because I was still traveling a lot, I was able to get prescriptions refilled easily. That slippery slope of depending on prescriptions really can come back to bite you. Fast forward to 2014. As long as I kept the medication at a high level, I was functioning. Still in a lot of pain, but functioning. I had had to divest myself of a number of my interests. I was in the process of selling off companies and land.

SHAUN: This is the pivotal moment when your life journey would be forever changed. Take us into the moments leading up to your out-of-body experience.

JIM: Yes. One evening in April, I had received a request from a company that was acting as my surveying company to go and look at a large tract of land that I was trying to sell and to make sure that the markers were in the correct place. I didn't drive much because of my medical condition, but it was all on back roads. So I got in my truck and drove to that field. It was late afternoon, early evening in springtime. And I managed to get to the field. When I drove into the field, I didn't plan it this way, but I was facing the setting sun, and I turned the truck off and sat there trying to get up the strength to make my way around this large piece of property and check the markers. I remember thinking, "Boy, I don't know if I can do this. That's a long way around."

I'd gotten into the habit of hiding medication so that my wife wouldn't see that I was overtaking it. I moved some things in the console of my truck and I saw some of the medication and a bottle of pop. And I thought, "Well, a few more. One won't hurt." Famous last words. I took them knowing full well that I had already taken far more that day than the prescription called for. And I sat back in the truck seat waiting for that warm relief that I had become accustomed to as the pain was dulled for a few hours. But as I sat there, something different started to happen. I remember the feeling of heat in my lower legs was so intense that I thought the truck must be on fire. I looked down quickly and there was no fire. And this raging heat came rushing up my legs, and then from my fingertips, inward toward my chest.

JIM: It came, as I said, from a place inside of me I hadn't been to in a long, long time. No sooner had I gotten the words out than I collapsed on the steering wheel and hit my head violently and I was gone. The next thing I was aware of was a tremendous pain on my forehead. I sat back up and I was in the truck looking out, and I knew time has passed because the sun was now on the horizon as it set. And then the realization flooded through me that I had no pain. The pain was gone. I finally got it right. You have to take the whole bottle.

I slid out of the truck and I walked about 15 to 20 feet away. I felt incredible. It was as though I'd taken off a heavy, wet overcoat and, with it, the pain. I felt like I was 16 again, and I was just overwhelmed and overjoyed. And I was looking out at the setting sun. I could hear the birds at springtime. I could smell the grass, and I was just overwhelmed that the medication finally worked. And then I turned and looked toward my truck.

And I was outraged. Someone was in my truck. Not only that, he had the audacity to be sleeping on my steering wheel. And so I turned to go over there and give him a good what-for. Have you ever had a dream where you're trying to run from something and it's as though your feet can't move? I realized that as hard as I tried, my feet would only move an inch or two at a time. I was stunned; I felt so good. Why couldn't I just run over there and grab this guy? I did make slow progress. And then I looked up and, gentlemen, the realization hit me that the man in the truck leaning over the steering wheel was no stranger. It was me.

SHAUN: Would it be an understatement to say you were shocked?

JIM: Shaun, my mind was trying to reconcile that I am here and yet I am there at the same time. How can this be? And of course, being a guy who could fix anything, in my arrogance I immediately concocted a scheme that if I could just get over there and get back in my body, everything would be okay. So I struggled to get over there. And I knew it was me because my head was turned this way on the steering wheel. There was blood gushing from my mouth and nose. I struggled to get closer to get back into my body, but suddenly I began to rise.

Now, as a pilot, I'm a good judge of altitude. And as I was rising, I was stunned because how could this be? I looked, and now I was drifting slowly backward, rising continuously. I could look down and see the bed of my truck, see my toolbox, and I was stunned.

I rose a little higher and then something made me look up instead of down, because I could see the surrounding area. I could look through the back window of the truck. I could see my body slumped over the wheel. And then I turned and I looked up, and there right in front of me was this golden circle. It was maybe 200 feet away. It was about 60 feet in diameter, and it was like the gold of a wedding ring. And then suddenly the center of it filled with a golden light. I had the impression that it swung inward and backward, like the door of an old-fashioned safe.

Immediately my body went into a reclining position of about 45 degrees. And I mean, unless you've lived under a rock in a cave, I think everyone has heard of the tunnel of light, but I never paid any attention to it. Suddenly I began to go forward toward this tunnel of light. As I went through the ring, I could see an immense distance. All of it was covered with a cloud that was golden, but there was a distinct path through the center. Once I realized what this was, it was as though I had pushed the throttles on an L-1011 forward to achieve V-1 on takeoff. I felt this tremendous force of speed. And I went at tremendous speed into this tunnel of light reclining backward about 45 degrees.

To give you an idea of the speed, I could feel and see the stars streaming by. I mentioned that in Baltimore one night, and there was a young guy in the front row and he said, "Sounds like the opening of *Star Trek* to me." That's a pretty good analogy. It was the stars streaming by. I was terrified because I'm a technical person, always understanding why things are happening, wanting to learn. But I was absolutely baffled. There was no rationale, no technical reason I could attach to this. The other thing that I remember vividly was that when you're going fast, whether you're in your convertible or in a speed boat or on your motorbike, you hear the rush of the wind. You hear the noise of the air. But right now? Nothing. Complete silence. And yet the sensation of tremendous speed.

I could feel and see the stars streaming by.

SHAUN: Many of our friends have reported seeing a light or a tunnel early on in their near-death experience. What did you encounter next?

JIM: I suddenly became aware of a bright light at the end of the tunnel that was even lighter than the tunnel. And as I came toward it, I decelerated and came upright. I found myself facing—I still don't know whether to call it a door or a portal covered in mist. But I did know I had no choice because I sensed that the tunnel was closing behind me. And so I stepped through this mist-covered portal and gingerly put one foot inside because I could not see what I was stepping onto. I felt something firm and brought my other foot in. I looked down as the mist started to clear and I was stunned because I was looking at the most perfect green grass I'd ever seen. Each blade was beautiful in its symmetry and its evenness. I now know what they mean by the grass is always greener on the other side. They're talking about heaven.

The mist cleared in front of me. I looked up and to my right, where this beautiful mist was lifting off this field. The field was covered in flowers of so many colors—colors that I have no name for. I've traveled to 52 countries in the world. I've been to the most beautiful places, but nothing compared to this. I was stunned by the beauty of it and the rolling fields that seemed to go on forever and this beautiful vault of a darker blue sky than we're used to here on earth—but no sun. As a pilot, I was trying to orient myself and I thought, "If I could find the sun, I'd know my southeast, southwest." No sun. Everything seemed to generate a light that created this fusion of color.

I swung my vision to the left. As I left that beautiful vista on the right, the grass went from green to brown to black to scorched. I was really taken by looking for the technical reason. Why would there be this dichotomy between these two vistas? The darkness continued to the left and into what seemed to be a crevasse. I guess I'm just naturally inquisitive. I made a few tentative steps to the left to see what was beyond this chasm. As I looked down, it was as though the walls of this chasm were covered with a shiny black anthracite coal. The first thing I saw at the very pit of the bottom of this abyss was a fire, a red fire, like a glimpse of a campfire in a distant valley.

But I was caught by the difference. Not only that, there was a sense of gloom, a miasma, a sense of dread. I think ever since we crawled out of caves, we've always feared the darkness. I started to turn away from this, but then something happened—the fire became greater at the bottom. As I was looking down, two things happened. The brightness of the fire increased, and I realized that down and looking sideways, it was as though a large door had opened and I could hear a sound for the first time. The sound was the sound of two large doors being forced open on hinges that had not been oiled. You could hear them screeching and so on, just rusty. That flooded the view with more light, and I realized the light was coming from the side to the bottom.

Then, to my utter amazement, something shuffled out of that doorway. The doorway was huge and so was the creature that came out. I looked down on it, and it appeared to have a form—large, round. It was on fire. Its body was on fire. Its head was squat on the shoulders and it seemed to be searching around the bottom of this pit for something. Suddenly it was as though it became aware of me, and it swiveled its head around and looked up at me. And fellows, I can tell you something—the look of hatred that I saw in its glowing eyes, not just for me but for all of mankind, will stay with me forever. On top of that, there was an odor that came out of that pit, a sense of decay, a sense of all things bad. As I said, a miasma.

There was screaming, and the screaming was not coming from its mouth. It was as though this creature had consumed souls and they were crying out for mercy.

SHAUN: It's hard to imagine a more terrifying encounter. What did you do?

JIM: I turned because I couldn't bear to look at it, but just the second before I turned, it began to scramble up the sides of that pit. Now, for its size—it was large—it moved with amazing nimbleness and crawled very rapidly up the side of that pit. And I scrambled backwards falling backward on my elbows, and it reared up out of the pit. I was confronted by this creature—body on fire, dripping saliva, and the most horrendous face. But the other thing was there was screaming, and the screaming was not coming from its mouth. The screaming appeared to be coming from within the body. Randy, it was as though this creature had consumed souls and they were crying out for mercy.

It stepped out of the pit and lumbered toward me. To keep my sanity, I scrambled to my feet and turned my back to it. Remember, I mentioned six words. I said the first three, "God, forgive me." Now I turned toward the beautiful light and I raised both hands. This time I cried out the next three words, three words that I had never prayed in my life: "God, help me."

I turned toward the beautiful light and I raised both hands. This time I cried out the next three words, three words that I had never prayed in my life: "God, help me."

Instantly, three points of light appeared in the beautiful cerulean blue sky, converging toward me. One was coming from about 90 degrees, the other one from about 260, and the other one from about 310, all converging into one. At the same time, this creature was behind me. And then, in addition to the screaming, I heard it speak my name. This creature knew me. It knew me. I wasn't that bad of a person. I may not have gone to church, but what did I do to deserve this? All these thoughts were racing through my mind. I gave to the poor if there was a tax break, but what did I do to deserve this? And it had a strange voice. It was in between a growl and a whisper. And I could hear it saying, "Jim, we are here for you. We are here for you. Join us. Come to us."

I honestly believe that had I turned at that moment and looked into its face, I would have been snatched, but instead I concentrated on this beautiful light coming toward me. All of a sudden, the lights fused together, and I was looking at this light traveling toward me and the light washed over me. At that point, I turned to look back. Randy, when that light struck that creature it screeched and screamed in agony and scrambled backward like a rat running for cover. Darkness and evil cannot live in the light of God. It must stop playing in the light of God.

SHAUN: That's a profound thought, both in heaven and here on earth. The light of God overpowers darkness.

JIM: I turned back to look. I might not have gone to church, but I knew what an angel was. And suddenly I was looking at three magnificent beings coming toward me—very tall, very elegant, silver long hair, beautiful golden light, which was, as I learned later, a refraction of their golden wings that creates what we call a halo. It's the light of their silver hair from their wings when their wings are extended. I remember being astonished because of the feeling of love and peace and safety that flooded over me was truly overwhelming, and just mere seconds before I felt all this hatred and evil toward me.

They came right up to me, and the first one approached me. And of all the things that I will always remember about this incredible encounter were their eyes. Now imagine these beautiful creatures—ten feet tall. Another one about 12 feet tall. And then the one coming behind dressed in warrior gear, truly a guardian angel, about 15 feet tall. These were wonderful creatures. The first one walked up to me and looked down at me. And the thing that I'll always remember is their violet eyes. Then he spoke to me and his lips didn't move. It was more than telepathy. He was in my mind and I was in his. And I say "he"—I don't want to use the word *androgynous*, but they looked like the best of all of us. They had the gentleness of a female and the strength of a warrior—just this incredible combination of everything that's good.

They had the gentleness of a female and the strength of a warrior— just this incredible combination of everything that's good.

All of a sudden, I felt this wonderful arm come up and around my shoulder. And then this magnificent, huge, feathered wing came out around his arm and he pressed me into his chest. And I looked up into those violet eyes and heard this beautiful voice in my mind that said to me, "Fear not, James, for we are your constant friends." And now as you gentlemen probably know, whenever you get an email or a text or a letter from me, I always sign it, "Your constant friend."

So there I was cuddled up to something that I thought was just a myth, a legend, and I felt so safe and warm. And I know we're running late, but I have to tell you this. As I was being hugged, I suddenly became aware of the incredible smell of warm tapioca. And I'm not here to start the church of the holy tapioca. I'm not, but here's something you should know, because you will all experience this. God knows what a huge difference to this is for us to encounter Him and His beings, and so He gives us something that we loved as a child to make us feel we have come home. And when I was a young boy walking home through a snowstorm in Northern Canada in the middle of June, I'd get to my grandmother's house and I'd go in and on her woodstove she would have made warm tapioca for me. Isn't that wonderful? And for some of you, it may be the smell of your mom's perfume. It might be any of those things that brought you joy as a child. For me, it was the smell of tapioca. So I don't mean to digress.

RANDY: I'll help you digress a little bit again, because for me when I met my grandmother in heaven, it was chocolate chip cookies.

JIM: Really?

RANDY: Yes, when I visited her home that's what I smelled, those chocolate chip cookies. That was the fragrance in heaven.

Jim, our audience has sometimes noted the variance in the stories—that is, each of us recounts things a little bit differently, or sometimes significantly differently than what others have mentioned. I know it doesn't bother you or me to hear these different accounts, because we each reach a destination. Along the way, our travels to that destination and even our expression of how that destination looks and appears to us is relevant to our own experiences or personality and all of those things. I just think it reflects the glory of God to know us and what we need.

Your account of meeting the creature I can identify with to some extent, having seen a battle between the angels and the demons as I was being pulled by that proverbial light. I thank you for bringing us to the account where you met the angels and the warmth of those angels and how they affected you, the three of them. But I've got to ask you this question, Jim, because I recall reading in your book that when you woke up, you mentioned to your wife, "There are horses in heaven." You've got to get to the horses, Jim, and what you saw there.

JIM: I apologize. I am guilty, as I said at the beginning of the conversation, of trying to get as much into the story as I can, because I'm afraid I'll leave something out that may help someone. So anyway, the guardians were wonderful. I felt safe. They were very elegant. I do have to tell you this, because I think people would be very interested in this. I was taken by how they bowed to me. They bowed to me, and I felt rather uncomfortable because I should be bowing to them. I wondered why, because it was such a very low bow of respect and subservience. And they spoke with this kind of Victorian perfection in their voice. I didn't hear any *thou* or *thee*, but a very measured tone that with every word they spoke there was incredible wisdom. I questioned the guardian that I eventually found out was mine all my life. That angel had pulled an awful tour of duty, but I digress. I asked why, and they said, "James, do you not know that when we look at mankind, we see the spark of life of our master?" Isn't that something? We who consider ourselves the lowest of the low are looked at by the angels, and they are in awe of us.

I'll skip forward—they showed the many things, told me many things. I'd developed 360-degree omnivision, I call it. I heard everything. I understood everything. The beautiful flowers spoke to me, sang to me. But eventually we came to this beautiful pasture, and I guess they knew my love of horses. And again, Randy, I think it ties into your comment on your grandmother's chocolate chip cookies and my love of tapioca. They wanted to show me something that would really make me happy. The second guardian raised his hand, and suddenly horses came from around the grove of trees toward me, and as they trotted across the grass, the grass lit up with the light from their hooves. Three of the most magnificent horses came toward me.

> *Three of the most magnificent horses came toward me.*

Now, I had never studied the Bible. I had no idea at that time that when Jesus comes back, He'll be riding a white horse. It's in the Bible. I was stunned, because as I stood there they came right up to the fence. I had loved their kind all my life, and they seemed to know that. They looked at me with such love in their eyes. And I reached forward to stroke the neck of the lead horse, and my hand sank right into the body of this being of light. And when I pulled it back, Randy, the light of the horse's body stuck to my hand until I got 10 to 12 inches away and then it went back into the horse's body. It was just phenomenal to watch and to experience. I've come to call it the sticky love of God, not something you hear every day. So those were the horses.

From there, they showed me more things. Suddenly, I was conscious of one of the guardians standing next to me. He said, "Hold my cloak." And so I reached over and held on and suddenly we were above looking down and I thought I was looking at a reflecting pool, but it opened up and I realized I was having an aerial tour of heaven. I hate using that term because you hear people talk about our experiences, Randy, and they call it *heavenly tourism*. You know what a lack of faith is in that term of derision. I believe with all my heart and know this is real. I wasn't imagining it. I wasn't hallucinating.

SHAUN: That's absolutely amazing. I love that God gave you a tour of heaven from an aerial perspective, a vantage point that you both loved and were familiar with.

JIM: I didn't know at that time that I wasn't being allowed to stay—you have to remember that. People have asked me, "Did you see your family?" No, I did not. It was explained to me later that I could not set foot in the heavenly city, but they would show me the heavenly city. I didn't connect it with the fact that I wasn't staying. I did see the halls of knowledge, the halls of wisdom, how heaven is laid out, and yes, the streets are gold, but it's not the brassy gold that we come to think of on earth. It's a different shimmer of gold. It's not the Fort Knox kind of gold. I saw many things and had the opportunity to ask many questions.

One thing I do want to talk about, because this is a comfort to so many parents. There was one building that stood out among all the rest, and the buildings are made, not of stone, not of wood, but of a material that has a light in it. Now I don't want it to sound to Las Vegas-y, but it was a gentle, welcoming light. This particular building glowed with a light that had a warmth to it. I asked what building that was, and I was stunned when they said, "That is the nursery."

I responded, "A nursery in heaven?"

They said, "Yes, James, the souls of aborted children or children who die in their innocence from disease come back here." Each soul is so precious to God that they're cared for. They grow at a different rate because they're not growing in a physical body. So they grow at about three times the rate that a child does on earth. This is where they take care of the little souls that were unwanted or died. I had no idea how this part of the story would have such an effect on women who have lost children or who had an abortion at a time in their life when they had no other option. It's been a blessing to explain to these parents that their child lives.

***This is where they take care of the
little souls that were unwanted
or died. Each soul is so precious
to God that they're cared for.***

Anyway, getting right to the main event—after showing me much more, we came back to the ground of paradise, which I learned was outside the walls. I was looking once again at the horses and I realized I hadn't seen my guardian for a while. So I turned to look for him and I saw him, and he was about 40 to 50 feet away on a small rise. When I looked, he was bent over almost in the kneeling position and was holding up a book, and facing him was a more magnificent figure than even the angels. But I couldn't see the face; it was in profile to me.

You know how you drive down a hot road on a warm summer day and there's a shimmer on the pavement? There was this kind of shimmer covering the features of this magnificent being, but clearly He was reading what the guardian was holding up. And I took note of the book that the guardian had taken out of his sleeve. It was as thin as a cheap roadside diner menu. And suddenly the awareness came over me that what the guardian was holding was the book of my life. Instead of it being a book filled with good deeds and kindness, all I had to show for a life that I thought was the epitome of success was this tiny, thin book. Charles Dickens wrote a wonderful line when he wrote, "Mankind should have been my business," Instead, it was all about the pursuit of wealth. And all I had to show for it, although I thought myself a kind person, all I had show for my life was this little thin book. I am determined to live my life now so that when I go back, when they open the book of my life for this chapter, they're going to need three angels and a forklift to get it open.

SHAUN: It's sobering to think about Jesus reviewing the book of our life that is recorded in heaven.

JIM: Yes. Anyway, I was watching and this figure was leaning forward, clearly intent on the little bit that was written in there. Suddenly the figure straightened up and the angel folded up the book, put it in his sleeve, and disappeared. And then this magnificent figure turned toward me. As He turned from profile to direct-on, suddenly the shimmer that had covered His features vanished. And I found myself face to face with none other than Jesus Christ, the Son of God—someone I thought was just some old Jewish legend that people had made up. I was looking at this figure and the magnificence of this figure. Not just the look of intense love and concern for me, but this golden light flowed out of Him. It seemed to start at His head and flow down His body. It was light that behaved like slow-moving water. It flowed off Him and it flowed down that slope. I fell to my knees and tried to crawl toward Him. I had to get closer. It was as though I had finally come home; I had found what I had searched for all my life. And I started to crawl toward Him to get closer. And then His eyes looked into mine. When I looked into those eyes of gray and green blue, I was lost in the love of eternity.

This magnificent creature knew me, too, but this was a creature of love and forgiveness and He desired to know me better. And Randy, you probably experienced this too. For a split second, although my intellect knew better, when my eyes met His it was as though I was the only one in creation, the only one He had ever created. He knew me that intimately and loved me that deeply. In that moment I knew from then on, whatever happened to me, I was His forever, but I just wanted to be around Him.

> *He knew me that intimately and loved me that deeply. In that moment I knew from then on, whatever happened to me, I was His forever, but I just wanted to be around Him.*

I tried to crawl closer to Him and two guardians appeared beside me and held me back. I struggled free and continued to climb toward Him. Suddenly He raised His right hand and there was no mistaking what the gesture meant. He was still smiling in a gentle way, but this was a definite command to stop. I remember the feeling inside of me of not being allowed to come closer. I waited with bated breath, I guess—if I was breathing. But I was just completely enveloped in the love of His eyes. And then I guess I must've taken another step or two or crawled on my knees. All of a sudden, He raised his hand even higher. And Randy, when He raised His hand, His cloak fell back and I saw the remains of the crucifixion. And then He looked intently at me and He began to speak to me.

People say to me, "What did He sound like?" How can I possibly be accurate? But suddenly I heard His voice. And with Him, unlike the angels, which was more of telepathy or a mental thing, Jesus' face moved just as you or I would when speaking to each other. And then I heard the voice of the Son of God, and it stunned me that He knew my name. He knew me.

He looked at me with the gentlest of smiles—hands still raised, meaning to not come forward. And He said to me, "James, My son, this is not yet your time. Go back and tell your brothers and sisters of the wonders we have shown you." And His hand slowly came down and crossed over His left.

I was overwhelmed with the fact that He knew my name, but more than that I was now coming to the realization that I wasn't being allowed to stay. And I began to plead. I began to beg, "Please let me stay. This is what I've yearned for all my existence. I just want to be wherever You are. Please don't send me away. Please let me stay." I remember saying this: "Please let me stay. I won't be any trouble." Can you imagine saying that to the Son of God? "I won't be any trouble!" But I was desperate.

I began to beg, "Please let me stay. This is what I've yearned for all my existence. I just want to be wherever You are. Please don't send me away. Please let me stay."

Suddenly two guardians appeared beside me and lifted me from the ground and turned me around and were carrying me back down the path. I wrenched my shoulder away to turn to beg one more time to be allowed to stay. Jesus was gone, but standing exactly in the place where He had stood was this magnificent warrior angel that had greeted me. All of a sudden he began to expand. He grew even taller than 15 feet, and he put his wings out to their full magnificence and they spread out and upward in this beautiful gold, and he was surrounded with light and the message was clear that he was barring the way forward for me.

Suddenly, I felt the angels hold me again. Everything went dark. I was in a black tunnel and I could hear water and it was cold and painful. I felt like I was descending a tremendous speed, but unlike the tunnel of light there was no beauty, just darkness. I was going down this steep descent.

They tell me that I scared the daylights out of the nurses because I had been triaged. They told my wife that there was no hope of me coming back—there was no brain activity, no sign of dreaming, no sign of hallucinating, nothing, and brain activity of course is the measure of death, not heartbeat. They had me hooked up to everything. There was complete failure of all my organs. The doctors had said to Lorraine that they would keep me hooked up until our children arrived to say goodbye. Then they would recommend that she pull the plug on the machinery that was pumping blood through my organs.

> *They tell me that I scared the daylights out of the nurses.*

Suddenly I sat up right and scared the daylights out of the nurse, as she told me later. I was screaming around all the tubes because I was intubated. They ran and got my wife and said, "Mrs. Woodford, come quickly." Lorraine's a nurse. She ran into the room and she couldn't believe it. She said my eyes were as big as saucers. I was trying to reorient from the beauty of heaven to lying on a gurney. She climbed up on the bed with me and started to cry. They were slowly watching my blood pressure come back to normal. All my organs started to operate again. Eventually they pulled the tube out so I could speak clearly. My throat was terribly sore and raw. I looked into my wife's pretty face, and I said, "Lorraine, I saw Jesus, and Jesus has horses." Of all the things I could have said to her: "Jesus has horses and I'm back."

SHAUN: Wow, there are so many directions we could go after everything you've shared. Why do you believe God sent you back? How are your mission and your calling different on this side of your heaven experience?

JIM: Just let me quickly tell you this—the words that Jesus said to me. *James*—He knew my name. *My Son*—He's the Father of us all. *This is not yet your time.* That implies to me that if I live a good life, there will be a time when I'll go back. *Go and tell*—which I'm doing with you now—*your brothers and sisters of the wonders we have shown you.* And that's what I try to do every day. And to the cynics out there, when they see me hawking a book—the funds from this book go to help all the poor we can find. There's not a lot, but we do what we can.

RANDY: That's another thing that has been noted by some of the audience. I, like Jim, have authored a book and people say that we're just taking advantage of the opportunity. That kind of discounts the story in itself. In reality, many of the accounts that we've heard are cases where either the author has reluctantly entered into writing a book or has been compelled by this edict that they felt from the Lord, saying, "You need to share this story." I don't know if I've run across a single one who is a born-again believer in Jesus Christ who has profited significantly through this process. It all goes back into the ministry. It all goes back to helping others.

JIM: Sadly, as we all know, there are people preaching who do it for money only. So the rest of us are tarred with that brush. I don't look for any of that. I don't want any of that, but we do want to help all we can.

RANDY: And Jim, your story gives glory to Jesus Christ, and that's what I think is the test of a true testimony that the Lord wants to be shared publicly in forms like this, as opposed to those who may share it and kind of give that glory to themselves. They feel enlightened or something to that effect. I share this because I know Jim. I actually have to say, Jim, that I've heard your story before and read your book, and I have an affinity for what you went through. There may be a few others as well who are just with you in that experience. That is, I have a *koinonia* relationship with what you've gone through, even though our accounts are varied. There is that very identifiable kind of feeling and gripping. I was tearing up when you were with Jesus; I couldn't hold it in. That to me personally testifies of the reality and also the need to tell this story publicly to give glory to the Lord of His reality and His truth and His love.

So, Jim, I just have one final question for you. You've touched on it before, but why do you think the Lord gave you this experience? Because not everybody does have this experience. Why do you think He gave it to you, especially you, and what have you done with it? Obviously, you've done a lot of good things with it, but what's your kind of central message that you want to convey to others?

JIM: You know, that's something I've often thought about. Why me? The first few times that I started to speak publicly about this, I said, "I have no idea why God chose me." And there was an older pastor in the front pew of the church, and he stood up immediately and he said, "Jim, why not you?" He said, "You will live a life of criticism, but none of that will matter because you are doing what God told you to do. Go and tell your brothers and sisters." So that's what drives me. And it was my friends at Destiny Image Publishers, whom I met through my coauthor, Thom Gardner, who convinced me really to do the book because I too had concerns about being perceived as someone who did this for money. And sadly, as I said earlier, there are people who do that. So coming back to your original question, Randy, I really don't know, but I'm trying to do the best job I can for God. When Jesus asks you to do something, man, you get filled with a feeling of power that you've never felt before. So I'm just doing what I was told.

When Jesus asks you to do something, man, you get filled with a feeling of power that you've never felt before.

SHAUN: And as you mentioned, Jim, there is that period of time between when the heart stops and the brain stops. It's a short period of time. The longest studies have shown up to six minutes, but no longer. Yours was hours.

JIM: Pardon me for interrupting. The reason it says 11 hours is based on the time that I was found and the time I resuscitated. In other words, the medical history, but time doesn't matter, you know this. Time's different there. Time exists, but it's different. I don't know if it was 11 hours, 11 years, or 11 seconds. All I know is that everything they wanted me to learn, I learned. And as I mentioned, the cynics sometimes make rude comments, but that's nothing compared to the hundreds of thousands who have reached out to me and said, "You helped me so much." You know? Just two nights ago, I had a gentleman call me, because I'm easy to get, and he said, "I want you to know I was prepared to end my life, and I saw you on a TV program as I was getting ready to go out the door to leap off a bridge." That is incredible. I hope that they have recorded that in heaven, so that next time the book of my life will be worth the time for Jesus to rate.

SHAUN: Wow, that's a powerful testimony to end on!

REFLECTIONS ON JIM WOODFORD'S EXPERIENCE

RANDY: What strikes me about Jim's story is his humility in sharing his afterlife encounter in striking contrast to the worldly perspective he embraced as the so-called "Diamond Jim" prior to meeting the angels. This afterlife encounter made him tenderhearted, and it turned his life to one of serving others versus serving himself. I really appreciate that about Jim's life change, post his Heaven encounter.

Certainly, the story of seeing the nursery in Heaven has touched a nerve in the public. People often wonder whether newborns or the unborn go to Heaven, and Jim's account confirms that, indeed, they do go to Heaven.

Jim learned about success in the world, but in Heaven Jim learned about a contradictory view of "success" from God's perspective. I think each of us can learn from Jim's experience that what matters to God is devotion to Him foremost, and then service to others. If we get that right, we will reap heavenly treasures. Jim embodies (or "disembodies") that truth extraordinarily well.

SHAUN: There are three things that really stuck out to me from Jim's story.

First was the specificity that he as a pilot was able to bring to describing the physics of the movement as he began rising towards heaven. Nobody else has been able to describe this part of their experience with such exactness.

Second, I was touched as were our viewers by the account of the nursery in heaven where all of the lost babies go. We've received numerous responses from our audience about how this healed a deep wound in their heart from a lost child.

Last, I have to make mention of the horses Jim encountered in heaven. This is significant, because it speaks to the reality of animals in heaven. We've had numerous guests who have shared with us about meeting their beloved pets, especially dogs in heaven. For Jim, encountering the horses was significant because they are one of his great loves and passions here on the earth. That just speaks to God's love, that he allows people to encounter the things that are dear to them in heaven.

FIND OUT MORE

If you'd like to encounter more of Jim Woodford's story, we encourage you to pick up a copy of his book *Heaven, an Unexpected Journey: One Man's Experience with Heaven, Angels, and the Afterlife* (Destiny Image, 2017). You can also connect with Jim at JimWoodfordMinistries.com.

THREE

LUNG TRANSPLANT RECIPIENT MIKE OLSEN DIED AND MET HIS ORGAN DONOR IN HEAVEN

MEET MIKE OLSEN

Louisville, Kentucky pastor Mike Olsen suffered for several years with idiopathic pulmonary fibrosis, a disease that kills almost as many patients as breast cancer. Mike was relieved when he received a call from the doctor letting him know that they had received a pair of lungs for him.

During his much-needed lung transplant surgery on January 7, 2019, tragedy struck when the last clamp was removed. Mike bled out, flat-lined, and was dead for a period of time.

He had many wonderful experiences on the other side of the veil, most notably meeting his organ donor! We pray Mike's heavenly encounter unveils new dimensions of God and fills your heart with the hope of heaven.

INTERVIEW WITH MIKE OLSEN

RANDY: Mike, it is such a pleasure to have you with us on the show today. We've been waiting a long time to hear your fascinating story, but let's start with your reason for having the lung transplant, how that came about, and your experience with Jesus Christ in heaven.

MIKE: Sure. So glad to be here guys, and yeah, what a journey it's been. In 2014, I was diagnosed with what's called idiopathic pulmonary fibrosis, which is a scarring of the lungs. They don't know what causes it. It's killing as many people as breast cancer. Before that, there was an ice storm here in Kentucky and I had pneumonia and think that kind of kicked it off. I was sick for about five years with this disease. I went and had a lung biopsy done to make sure that's really what it was. After the biopsy, I was put on oxygen 24/7. So I had two of what we call E-tanks that I was dragging around behind me for quite a long time.

I got on the transplant list, but I had to wait a very long time on that list. So as I was waiting on that list, my wife and I were doing a lot of public awareness to bring awareness to this lung disease that nobody knows about. I was meeting with politicians and celebrities and doing anything I could do to get the word out about this disease. Now I'm a preacher—I believe in signs, wonders, and miracles. God can do anything He wants. Yet I had come down with this disease and I said, "Well, I could be bitter about this or be better at this." So I decided to be better and be proactive in what was going on. So I used to meet with lung patients when they called. I tried to, you know, just be there for them online in the different support groups for lung disease.

So anyway, I got a call one time and a friend named Mary said, "Hey, I'm in the area. I'm going to be at this state park and I was wondering if you'd come to meet me. I like to meet face to face." I said sure. So we went over there and we met and we had a really good time. My wife, unbeknownst to me, was struggling with the fact that I had a terminal lung disease. As we were driving home late at night, she started singing this song by John Michael Talbot: "Father, I Place My Life in Your Hands." As we were driving down the road, this is what she told me she was doing. She was lifting all her burdens to heaven and saying, "I can't handle this. Financially, physically, emotionally, all these things that are going on with Mike."

She started lifting them up in the car, like taking them in her hands and just placing them in God's hands, saying, "You take this; this is too much." So she started singing, "Father, I place my life in Your hands."

I joined her; we were driving 55 miles per hour down the highway. All of a sudden, right in front of us this deer appeared out of nowhere. I slammed on my brakes and we both just cried out, "Jesus!" You know, I thought, *I'm not going to die from terminal lung disease. I'm going to die from this deer coming through the windshield.* So when we cried out this deer was like 12 inches from the bumper.

We had no other choice but to brace for impact. And all of a sudden this deer disappeared into thin air. We looked at each other, shaking. We stopped on the highway and looked behind us. I was like, "Where did this thing go? Where did it go?"

We had no other choice but to brace for impact. And all of a sudden this deer disappeared into thin air.

We drove home and for the first day or so we were baffled, like, what was that? I mean, it was like a *Star Trek* episode. I mean, this thing appeared, dematerialized, and just wasn't there anymore. So being the Bible student I was, I started thinking of scriptures, like, what does this deer mean? I thought of the scripture that says "as the deer pants for the water so my soul pants after You, God." Well, that didn't fit. Then I called my son because he is an Irish dancer and his nickname is "leaping deer." A guy at a service one time called him out and gave him that nickname. So I called my son. I said, "Hey, did God show you anything lately, or have any kind of deer come in your pathway?

He said, "No, Dad, I don't see visions."

I said, "Okay. All right, just checking, son," and got off the phone.

All of a sudden it was like an epiphany in my mind. I thought, "Wait a second. I remember studying the tribes of Israel in Bible college." I remembered they had banners all around their camp with signals—like signs, images. And one of the images was a deer.

So I looked it up and the deer symbol was the tribe of Naphtali. In the story of Rachel and Leah, one could have a child and one couldn't. And the Lord said to Rachel, "I have seen your struggle." All of a sudden I thought, "Oh my goodness, that's why we saw this deer." Got it. God answered our prayer. He saw that we were struggling, not in our faith, but in our emotions and in knowing that I was dying. That's the kind of God I serve. To me, that's natural Christianity—that God would send a sign like that to encourage us, to say it's okay. That happened six months before I got the call for the transplant.

SHAUN: Mike, I love that God gave you a confirmation of Him being aware of your struggle to help you get through those long months of waiting for a transplant.

MIKE: He did, He was. So fast forward—I was diagnosed with this terminal lung disease, though I had never smoked. So I was really like, "Wow, how did this happen?" I was diagnosed with IPF, idiopathic pulmonary fibrosis, and I started getting weak pretty quickly. My oxygen needed to be increased, and I was just running out of time. So as I said, I was doing some awareness meeting with people. How I did that I have no idea, because I was so weak, but I did it anyway. It came up to the time I finally got a call. I was in my backyard, out in the cabin, and I was working on my folk art. I heard the Lord's voice saying, "You put that stuff up. You need to go now. You just put all that stuff up." Wow, that's kind of weird, but I heard His voice saying to do that.

So I put it all up, got back to the house, and my wife said, "The hospital's on the call. They have a pair of lungs for you." After waiting a very long time on the transplant list, I thought, "Wow, this is incredible." So we went to the hospital and I thought everything was going to be hunky-dory. I thought, "Man this is worth the wait. And God already told me ahead of time."

A lot of people were praying for me, saying, "We're going to believe for a miracle. And we're going to believe in supernatural lungs to come to you." Interesting enough, we had a friend who came over a couple of days before the Lord spoke to me to go back into the house. I had never met her. My wife knew her from work and she came. They said they wanted to pray for me. So I said, "Sure." So they came over and out of the blue this lady just said, "You're going to think I'm crazy, but I just saw a vision of a pair of lungs coming down from heaven and being put into your chest." She had no clue. She didn't know I was going to get a call for a transplant a couple of days later.

Anyway, sure enough I got the call. I went to the hospital, got prepped, and got wheeled into the OR. For the first hour or so, things were going okay. My wife went home because we lived 15 minutes from the hospital, and she went home to sleep. It was like a 12-hour surgery. All of a sudden, one of my oxygen tanks on the front porch fell over. *Boing!* You know, these things are loud when they fall. My wife woke up, like, "What? That's never happened in all the years we've had these oxygen tanks stored on the front porch." So she called the hospital and they said the first lung was in. So she thought, "Wow, okay, God woke me up to let me know the first lung is in."

I bled out. I died on the table.

After that, the second lung went in, and as they were closing me up, the doctor took the clamp off too early. And I bled out. I died on the table. So in that situation, they were trying to get me back to life. They transfused me with a bunch of blood. But during that time, I saw myself rising off the operating table.

I'm a jokester. So I just said to myself, "Well, at least I'm going up." You know, because that's a good thing. So now, as a pastor, I had the assurance. I knew the scriptures. I knew that I would be going to heaven if I ever died, but I just found it kind of comforting to know I was rising off the table. But as I got off the table, all of a sudden I heard all these negative voices, and they were saying, "You're not good enough. Who do you think you are?" And just taunting me. I thought, "Well, I know what that voice is." And I said, "In the name of Jesus, leave me alone and shut up because I'm a child of God and you can't say those things," and all those voices silenced and never spoke again.

*I just said to myself,
"Well, at least I'm going up."*

This is where I get emotional. So as I was rising off the table, further toward the ceiling, I saw these rainbow lights swirling all around me. I was like, "Wow, what is this?" I was trying to discern—I still had my mental faculties, so I was trying to discern, "Is this the medicine? What is this?" And then these bright rainbow lights started singing. And then I knew it was angels. And I saw myriads of angels and they were singing, "Mike's coming home, Mike's coming home." They were so happy. And then I heard a voice saying, "No, he's just here for a visit." And as I rose into this bright light, I was just overwhelmed. I was like, "I'm standing in heaven." As far as the eye can see, it's bright light.

It was just a feeling of total bliss, total. Like I can't explain. I just felt like I was engulfed in light. And then I started thinking about things in my life that I had done. And it was like, that realization came right there in heaven, and it was like, "It's all taken care of, Mike." And then the thought came, "Jesus is all in all." Every molecule, I felt His presence throughout this expanse.

SHAUN: Did you realize anything profound as you were engulfed by God's presence?

MIKE: I thought, "Oh my goodness. I worried about way too much stuff on the earth." I was worried about my finances. I was worried about my health. Even as a Christian, I was worried about my spiritual condition—did I do enough? You know, was I good enough? I knew Jesus took care of it. But when I got there, He did take care of it. It was like the slate was washed clean. The realization was, "Mike, it's not you anyway. Why, why were you even thinking that? It's all Jesus." I mean, the whole place was filled with His presence. The glory of the Lord fills the temple—that was the Lord.

As I stood there, all of a sudden I got emotional. I started thinking about the donor. I thought, "Oh my God, this guy died so that I could live. This guy died so I could have his lungs." I thought I'd said it out loud, but I think it was in my spirit man, because in heaven when I was talking back and forth, it wasn't like speaking. It was like, my spirit was speaking, I guess.

So anyway, I cried out through my spirit and I said, "I want to thank my donor." All of a sudden, I looked behind. I don't know why. I just felt a presence behind me. I looked over my left shoulder and there was Jesus, and there was the donor. How did I know it was the donor? I just knew. It was as if Jesus said, "Here he or she is." I don't remember. The figures were like, I couldn't see them fully, even Jesus. I don't know why that was. Anyway, the Lord came up to me and He put His hand on my left shoulder and He said, "Mike, these are your new lungs because you just received them."

I said, "Yes, Lord." And at that moment, when I said, "yes, Lord," I started floating back down to the OR table. I just had the feeling that I had to agree with Him. I had to agree that I would take this person's organ into my life, into my body. As a transplant patient it's so strange to even think about having somebody else's organ in your body. So God gave me the comfort to know that He knows about it. He knew about it before I'd even got the transplant done. He knew all things.

SHAUN: That's absolutely stunning. You're the only person we've talked to so far who has encountered their organ donor in heaven. What a privilege!

MIKE: Well, I came back and let me tell you what happened. I came back into my body and I didn't remember anything. I was in a coma for 10 days. My wife was at home and they discovered mold in the house. Well, that would do me in as a transplant patient. So she had to take care of all that, gut the bathroom, and do everything to get it ready for me.

During those first few days, my wife Patty was sitting and talking with her sister, Kay. She all of a sudden said, "Kay, I don't know how I know this, but Mike's in heaven right now, thanking his donor. I don't even know how I know that. I just know it like this, something I just know deep inside."

Her sister said, "Well, we'll see when he gets out of the coma."

Then one of our friends, Jonathan, who lives 45 minutes away from our house, called my wife several days later. He called and told my wife, "I was in my bedroom, and I got woken up by an audible voice of God in my room." The voice said, "Mike is with Me." He said, "I was so startled. And I didn't want to call you because I didn't want to, you know, let you know that he's dead." So he waited. Several days after that, he got another awakening out of sleep, and the Lord said, "He's back. He was with Me." So he told my wife this.

The voice said, "Mike is with Me."

Well, I was in a coma. So it kind of confirmed what she already knew. Then we had a friend who was a doubting Thomas—his name is Jeff. Jeff heard about me being in heaven, thanking my donor. He goes, "Listen, when Mike comes out of the coma and he's in ICU and they take the intubation tube out of his throat, I want to be there."

So she said, "Okay, Jeff."

So ten days went by. They took the ventilator tube out of my throat. Jeff came in and said to my wife, Patty, "Don't say anything. I want to speak first." So he came up to my bed and the nurse had just taken the tube out of my throat. I was talking like three octaves lower because I hadn't talked in over ten days; I was in a coma. So Jeff goes, "Mike, when you were out in the nether regions, did you experience anything?"

I mustered up strength enough to get my first words out of my mouth, and I said, "Yes, I went to heaven and I got to thank my donor." When I said that, my wife's eyes were just overwhelmed. She told Jeff, "I told you, I told you, he went to heaven and thanked his donor."

And Jeff said, "You were right, Patty." And I was nodding my head. I'm like, yep. That's what happened.

SHAUN: Did you have a sense that God sent you back with a specific purpose or message?

MIKE: You know, I just feel like I came back with a message to tell people. You hear about people saying, "Don't sweat the small stuff." That's kind of what it comes back to with this message. Even as Christians—man, trust God! I mean, He's got everything orchestrated—everything in our life. He knows what's going to go on in our life. He knows ahead of us. He knows it and he orchestrates angelic beings on our behalf to orchestrate things to happen the way they do. So I came back and I guess I just don't worry.

I came down with COVID this past January. Now listen, COVID would kill somebody like me who is immune suppressed, who had lung surgery, right? But you know what? During that whole time, I went and got the antibody infusion, but mainly I stayed out of the hospital because I thought, "These guys will kill me if I go in." So I got the infusion and went back to my bed and I was in bed for three weeks. But you know what? After that experience in heaven, I thought this was nothing. Do you know what I mean? God's mercy. Like, He's got this. I'm not going to die from this. I will not die from this. And God knows.

> *After that experience in heaven, I thought this was nothing. God's mercy got this. I'm not going to die from this.*

By the way, after my transplant, I got home and was lying in bed recuperating after 64 stitches across my chest. You know they break the rib cage open to go in and get the lungs. So anyway, I was in my bedroom and my wife was at work and I was just lying there trying to recuperate. All of a sudden, I opened my eyes and an angel was standing in my room, tall as the ceiling to the floor, and just staring at me. So I said out loud, "What is this, Lord?"

And the Lord said, "They're just watching you. They're just there. They keep watching you. They haven't left you since heaven."

I thought that was amazing. I mean, it is amazing that we read about these stories in the Bible and we just think, "Well, that's a nice story." Even angels appearing to Joseph in a dream, we think, "That happened then, but will it happen now?" Yeah, it will, and God continues to do things like that. We just need to believe that He is much bigger than our problems, much bigger than what we go through. It's just been an incredible journey.

SHAUN: I know God sometimes directs people to delay sharing their heavenly experiences for a time. When did you feel released to begin sharing your story?

MIKE: Just telling my story to you guys, I mean, I didn't go out and tell my story. I'm not that type of person who wants everyone to look to me. I just I want them to see the Lord in my life. But one day the Lord said, "You need to start sharing your heaven testimony." And I said, "Okay, Lord." I began sharing it with nurses because I went to the hospital every month to do blood work and things. I've also been sharing it with, I don't know, people on the street, you know. It's kind of weird, but I just started sharing and people would just break down and weep.

I met this one lady at a hotel. My sister-in-law was in the hospital and we were visiting her, and I was at the hotel. The lady said, "I see you have a service dog with you."

I said, "Yeah, I just had a double lung transplant, but I died and went to heaven."

And she said, "Tell me more." So I did, and she just started weeping. She goes, "You know what? I was struggling with heaven. Is it real? Is God real? Man, you coming to see me today at the front desk here and tell me that story. I am so at peace now. It's not going to bother me anymore."

You know, we overcome the enemy by the word of our testimony and by the blood of the Lamb. And I just believe that's what I've been doing—just sharing the testimony.

Every one of us has a story. And of course, people with NDEs have a story, and it might seem strange to people and almost unbelievable that these things happen. But you know what? I'm still engaged in heaven. I mean, every time I tell the story it's almost like I relive it and I have the same feelings as when I was in heaven. It just shows what an awesome God—that He allows these things to happen to us to assure us, assure everybody that there's a place called heaven. And He wants you to go there.

I tell people, I was brought up in a religious household, so we kind of knew all the stories of Jesus. I was raised Catholic, so I knew all about Jesus in my head, but He hadn't reached my heart. When I was a young man, I think 19, I just simply said, "God, if You're real, show me who You are." And believe me, He did. I asked Him to come into my heart, change my life, do whatever He needed to do. And man, I was radically changed from the person I used to be, and it was all His doing. And He's shown Himself faithful throughout all these years. He knew that I was going to have trouble with my lungs down the road and that I was going to have a terminal illness. He knew that already. And He already kind of went before me and lined things up.

I just simply said, "God, if You're real, show me who You are."

SHAUN: A couple of comments I'll throw out. So in terms of all the people that we've interviewed so far, Mike is our second closest to his near-death experience. We had another woman who was about a year out from her near-death or afterlife experience. Mike, you're about two and a half years out. It's interesting to me to be able to talk to somebody who is not as far removed from their experiences. Also in terms of that spirit-to-spirit communication, we pretty much get that from every single person we've talked to, where there was almost like a knowing or you didn't have to talk, you could just understand and converse.

What I'm curious to hear about—going into this experience, you were a charismatic Anglican priest. That's a bunch of words to fit together. So you were a pastor; you came from a Christian background before having your near-death experience. That hasn't been everybody's circumstance heading into their experience. But now, on the other side of the journey, how has your spiritual walk shifted? Many of the people we've talked with say they feel like they always have a foot in heaven. Like there's still a deep, constant connection to what they experienced on the other side.

LUNG TRANSPLANT RECIPIENT MIKE OLSEN DIED AND MET HIS ORGAN DONOR IN HEAVEN

So for you, how does your daily walk with the Lord look different on this part of your journey? I've never asked anybody that before, so I'm kind of curious.

MIKE: Well, you know, I was dubbed the hippie priest because I wore the robes and the clerical collar, but yeah, I danced a lot and raised my hands a lot. So I was probably an anomaly in the church, but I also was an Assembly of God pastor before I became a priest. So that kind of blew people's minds anyway. So what happened was I retired from ministry when I got deathly ill, when I couldn't stand in the pulpit any longer. It was a heartache for me because we had a great little church, and we just love ministering. We did missionary work. We did a lot of things like that, but after my heavenly experience things changed. I thought I was going to go back into ministry or do something after my transplant, but God had other plans.

We always have to go with the plans that God lays out. So things were different. Like I would be in groups of people whom I would never normally hang out with. God was putting me in these situations that were uncomfortable, and I'm like, "What do I do?" But it's so funny because I just had this chill attitude after being in heaven, and I was just like, "Everything's okay." I didn't have to be super spiritual or super religious. It's almost like that was lifted off of me. Not that I was before, but you've got to admit sometimes Christians can be a little judgmental or a little religious. I don't care what church you go to—you can fall into that trap.

I find myself just being me and letting the Lord work through me, through my experience. I know it was such a blessing, in a way, that I died because it's opened doors for me to share my story in different avenues and to let people know, you know, it's okay. It's okay that you're suffering. It's okay. I mean, it's not okay, but it's okay that you can talk about it. Normally, you know, as Christians we want to always have the answers. This is what the scriptures say, and this is how it should be. But I've learned to listen more since my heavenly experience. Seriously, just listen to people, let them talk, let them share their story and their experiences of life.

So now I think my ministry has switched to just being there. I've heard this quote from someone this week: "To be a witness is really to be with someone, a with-ness"—be there, be present in people's lives. I think when we have these NDE experiences, I don't want to say this to be proud or boastful, but I feel like I've been touched by heaven and that's an awesome responsibility. And I feel like I just want to give that to people. I want to give what I've been given from heaven to other people.

I felt like that when my sister-in-law was dying in the hospital. Part of me was like, "Come on, you're going to be healed." And then another part of me was like, "You know what? God's got her in the palm of His hands." So I was just present there with her, and I think that is important to be with people—weep with those who weep, right? Rejoice when they're rejoicing and just to be a real heaven ambassador to people, you know, to be there.

When I came to know the Lord myself, a lot of it happened in my bedroom. I went to churches and, yeah, I went to the altar and I did some things, but most of my encounters with God happened in a personal way, walking in the woods or something. When I went to heaven, I came back and I thought, "You know what? I think I made things too hard." You know, I think God's got it. I don't need to help Him as much as I thought He needed me to help Him. And I think He's always reaching out to men. He's always reaching to show His love, His mercy. And I just believe that, and I'm just a vessel.

He's always reaching out to men. He's always reaching to show His love, His mercy. And I just believe that, and I'm just a vessel.

Now I say, "God, what do You want me to do? You want me to be a motivational speaker? What do You want me to do?" So I'm just listening to Him every day and doing what I can. And then doors opened for me. I had Mike Huckabee call me and say, "Hey, I'm making you a Huck's Hero. Can you come down to Nashville and be on my TV show?" Like, sure.

Then I had a documentary made of my story by a news station here in Louisville. They followed me around for a year. And here's the funny thing. My story won an Emmy award. The funny thing about that was I was an actor in New York in musical theater. I gave that up when I was 19 to be in the ministry, and like 30, 35 years later, I'm walking the red carpet with this newscaster. And he hands me the Emmy award and he says, "This is yours."

You know I tease, so I said, "It took dying to get noticed around here." But seriously, I looked up to Him and I said, "God, You have a sense of humor." He always turns things for our good. It may take a little longer than we expected, but He always does. So when I go in my living room, I look at this Emmy award and I just chuckle because it's engraved, *I'm Dying Will You Help?* which is my story. And I just laugh because I'm like, "Oh, I'm just like a little podunk pastor in Kentucky with an Emmy award." Who does that? God does that.

RANDY: Mike you're a walking miracle. One of the things we talked about before the show was just how you've been able to minister to others. And as we've exchanged on Facebook, you've recently had some challenges with pneumonia. You mentioned COVID, actually, that you contracted, which for somebody who is immune suppressed that typically doesn't end well. What I find intriguing about your story and encounter in heaven is that you wanted to meet your donor. I've learned in the brief interactions on social media and the like that you have a tender heart toward other people. And I've heard this from other donor recipients that they're very thankful for the donor, but the Lord gave you this sight of your donor in heaven. Have you followed up at all since that time to express that gratitude?

MIKE: Yes. You know, we transplant patients are encouraged to write the donors' families, and I have twice, but sometimes the pain is so unbearable that it takes a while for them to write back. They have received my letters. They know that I'm interested in meeting them, and I can't wait to meet them because I want to share with them that their loved one was in heaven. I think that would mean a lot to them. And so I'm waiting for that day and praying that that would happen. So I did reach out to them and I'm hoping for that day to come.

SHAUN: Randy, if you have another question to throw in there, I'll let you get a second one in if you'd like, sir. I've got more, but I don't want you to miss out.

RANDY: You know, since we've done this series I have a kindred feeling, Mike and Shaun, with others who have had such encounters. They are all different experiences, but much the same. Mike, you and I met the Lord as believers. But one of the things that I discovered was that, for me, my faith before this was more of a hope rather than a conviction. And that conviction that comes through the experience is obvious. When you have an encounter like this, how can you not believe it? I feel like I was the doubting Thomas, and Jesus held out His hand and said, "Go ahead and touch My hand," where the crucifixion had occurred. So Mike, you came back having been a pastor and having ministered to others. I'm curious as to how your ministry to others compares, from being a pastor who preached the word of God to now being a pastor who has met the Word of God. How did that translate for you in your pastorship and ministry to others?

MIKE: Well, you know, I prayed as a pastor. I preached things from the pulpit from the Word of God, and I believed in what I experienced, but this is a whole new ball game. When you are in the presence of Jesus and heaven and come back, it's like the scripture where it says, "Didn't our hearts burn within us as we were in His presence?" That's kind of how it is for me now—I just want everyone to know how much God loves them deeply. And that's what I try to convey. Maybe I'm not in the pulpit now, but now I have other avenues that I'm using to convey that message.

We are so tunnel-visioned, as human beings, about our life experiences and how all that affects us. But my focus now is to let people know—God loves you deeply. God understands even your shortcomings, even your failures. A lot of people just give up because they think, "I'm never going to be good enough" or "I'm never going to overcome the situation or forgive people," you know? I just don't think they understand the mercy that God affords us if we just let Him work in our everyday lives, in our everyday circumstances. Just to see Him high and lifted up, you know, who He is—a high King of heaven.

Maybe we have misconceptions about who God is. I've seen Him as that authoritative figure with a bat in His hand, ready to bop us one because we've messed up. People just have a lot of weird ideas about God, but I feel like, after my experience, I have a lot more compassion to tell you the truth.

People just have a lot of weird ideas about God, but I feel like, after my experience, I have a lot more compassion to tell you the truth.

I'll tell you this one story. It's happened to me often since I've been to heaven. In the past, when I would see someone on the street, like beggars on the side of the highway, my attitude used to be like, "Come on, dude, you've got brand new sneakers on and a brand new backpack. You're not fooling me. You want this money for drugs." I was just, you know, a little judgmental and little sarcastic. After I came back, I started looking at the people maybe as God would see them. Even if they're shysters, why are they there? Why are they doing that? What brought them to that place?

If we would only see people through God's eyes. Yeah, there could be people who are annoying you today. People who are just making your skin crawl, or maybe certain people whom you see in the news who make you say, "Oh man, God, can You not take care of this situation?" We need to see things through God's perspective and we need to see things in the light of eternity. What's taking place here with my neighbor? What's taking place with the cashier at the store? If we could just be sensitive to them. I try to smile a lot. I mean, that's my M-O. I smile. I engage, even if just for a moment, with a cashier at the supermarket. I'm given a moment in time with a person and I want to make sure in that moment that they feel validated, they feel loved, and I always share something about my life, something about heaven. Something about the Father heart of God, so they can think about their own life. And when I share what I've been through, which I find myself sharing a lot, I think it brings hope. And one thing we need in this world right now is hope.

SHAUN: Yeah. I'll give that an amen. We need a lot of hope in this season, but as the world grows continually darker, I feel like that want, that need of hope only exposes how much more we need Jesus in our lives. While it's dark, it's challenging. I feel like that's also a hopeful aspect of the season that we're walking through. And Mike, we've had other guests talk about how, being in heaven, they're in an environment that's just saturated in love and they're immersed in love and they come back shifted and changed. Clearly, that's shifted your perspective with how you see people. It almost sounds like you're able to see people with the eyes of Jesus. You're able to view people kind of through that lens of love that Jesus has for us. And I just really appreciate you sharing that.

You know, when we start talking about near-death experiences, out-of-body experiences, all the different things, it attracts a wide range of viewers and listeners, some who grew up in church, some who came to faith later in life, but others who are just interested in the paranormal or supernatural. Maybe they've never darkened the door of a church. And for the person who is far away from Jesus, who maybe doesn't have any idea who He is, what would be your invitation to them? We know that Jesus wants to meet them, and Jesus wants to impact their life just as much as He's impacted the lives of all three of us.

MIKE: You know, I've done some interviews and looked at the comments afterward and some people didn't like the Christian aspect of my journey. And I would just tell them, or anybody, God is love. In Him is the fullness of love. If you're searching, ask Him—He wants us to ask questions. He just wants us to say, "Who are You? Who is this Jesus Mike's talking about? Who is this?" I don't want another religion. I always tell people, I don't have a religion. I have a relationship. That's the best thing—not to minimize God on my level, but He's a friend who sticks closer than a brother.

You know, I talk to God, of course, every day. I talk to Him even in all my struggles and every situation that I go through. I just talk to Him like a friend, like, "God, I'm struggling here." I'm not perfect. My halo isn't above my head; I'm still a work in progress. So I just try to tell people, even if they're not believers, listen—do you ever consider that maybe God has a plan in everything that you're going through? I try to kind of point them heavenward.

God can work. I believe God works through every person. He's always reaching out. He's a God who's always forward-thinking, looking toward us, and wanting the best for us. When I have people who maybe don't believe in Jesus, I say, you know what? I know you're struggling with that thought, but God loves you. Start with that. God loves you. And consider that Jesus was more than a prophet. What we do and what Christianity has—

put it out there. Consider who He was and look at His teachings and look at His life, you know? So I try to direct them in that way.

The bottom line is, we're living examples. We should be living examples every day. I've heard this time and time again—you kind of start acting like who you hang around with. And I hang around with Jesus. So hopefully, He's rubbing off on me and I'm rubbing off on others, you know? That's what I hope. I can only hope that my life made a difference here on the earth, that I made an influence for the kingdom of God, and that people see the joy of the kingdom. That's one thing that's undeniable—there's joy in the kingdom of God and there's peace. And man, if that experience in heaven showed me anything, wow, I mean, I want everyone to experience that. That's why I share the story. You've just got to go there. I don't want you to die to go there, but I'm just saying you've got to be in the presence of Jesus. When I was there, He filled all in all, and you know what? He could do that for you right here on earth. It's just a prayer away, you know? And I just said, "God, if You're real, Jesus, if You're real, make Yourself known to me." And that's what I tell people—try Him out. You'll never regret it.

---

*You've just got to go there.
I don't want you to die to go there,
but I'm just saying you've got to
be in the presence of Jesus.*

LUNG TRANSPLANT RECIPIENT MIKE OLSEN DIED AND MET HIS ORGAN DONOR IN HEAVEN

RANDY: Mike, you have spoken to so many hearts, people who just are struggling today. This seems to be an era, a time when many people are going through pain, suffering, and doubt. And you're assuaging many of those with just the genuineness of who Christ is. And I know that we pay tribute to God as a God of love. You're expressing that in a way that is sincere because you've had that encounter with love Himself. So we so much appreciate you being a part of this program. I know that our listeners and viewers have been greatly blessed, and we thank you immensely for being with us.

MIKE: I appreciate you having me. You know, I haven't told my personal testimony, but I came from a very abusive background and a lot of sexual abuse when I was younger. When I met Jesus, He set me free from all the wounding. So when I went to heaven, to just feel that the slate was washed clean. And I knew that here on earth, I knew that through scripture, but when I got to heaven and that feeling of being bathed in his light—that's what I want to tell people. You might have been through horrendous things in your life. You might've been through unspeakable things, but you know what? God was there with you. No, He didn't like what you went through, but He was there. He's guiding you out into the light.

SHAUN: Amen. Mike, thank you so much for sharing your amazing journey, your powerful story. I know for some of our listeners and viewers, maybe this conversation challenged you. I know it encouraged you, either way.

REFLECTIONS ON MIKE OLSEN'S EXPERIENCE

RANDY: Mike and I share a similar malady in that each of us clinically died because of lung disease. But what is so outstanding about Mike's experience is that he was introduced to his donor in Heaven. That to me speaks of God's Love in that God gave Mike the gift of knowing that his donor received a great reward in Heaven while Mike received his reward (new lungs) in this world. Through this experience God assuaged any guilt Mike may have experienced in being the beneficiary of a man who tragically lost his life.

Mike was also a pastor who, like others in this book, struggled with sin. His transparency is refreshing in that Mike shares about God's grace with a genuine appreciation of new life, both physically and spiritually through Christ's forgiveness.

Mike and I have gotten to know each other, and this reinforced my understanding of Mike as a changed man. I know that may sound cliché, but for Mike, change is more than a perfunctory altering of behavior. Mike operates in the spiritual realm today as easily as he does the physical realm, and that kind of transformation can only happen from a deep encounter with Jesus.

SHAUN: There are so many things I loved from Mike's experience, which made it hard to narrow it down to the top three that really stood out to me.

I appreciated the way Mike described how aware he was at the beginning of his out-of-body experience. Many of the men and women we've talked to have reported being aware of their surroundings and what was happening with their body as they were in the process of leaving it. It is very common for people to share with us that they had their full mental faculties and awareness when they were in either heaven or in hell.

The big thing that stands out in Mike's story is that he actually encountered his organ donor in heaven. He's the only person who has shared something like that with us. It's truly a sweet part of his journey, which I hope he's able to share some day with the family of his donor.

Last, I want to touch on how Mike saw angels after he was back on earth and recovering at home. Many of the men and women we've talked to report having a heightened sense of spiritual awareness after their afterlife encounter, where they're able to see in the spirit and are aware of angels, demons, and sometimes able to discern what is happening with other people (health issues, what's happening related to them in the spirit realm, etc.).

FIND OUT MORE

You can connect with Mike Olsen at www.facebook.com/Mike-Olsen-Project-179664296283994.

FOUR

IVAN TUTTLE DIED AND ENCOUNTERED SATAN IN HELL BEFORE SEEING GOD IN HEAVEN

MEET IVAN TUTTLE

In 1978, Ivan Tuttle was living a carefree life, going from one party to the next, from one high to another—when his fun, free life was interrupted by a pain in his leg. Doctors told him he had a dangerous blood clot—but Ivan didn't pay much attention to that. He was 26 and felt fine; blood clots were a problem for his grandfather, not him. Then the clock ran out.

What Ivan experienced next was like something out of a horror film. First, decaying demons tried to consume Ivan. Then he saw another figure unlike the others—it was satan. Ivan was struggling to get free when the Spirit of God emerged, telling him that the longtime prayers of his mother had been heard, and suddenly Ivan found himself transported into heaven. He experienced many wonders in heaven and was sent back to earth with quite a story to tell.

We know you'll be both amazed and inspired by his powerful testimony.

INTERVIEW WITH IVAN TUTTLE

SHAUN: I start most of my interviews by asking the guest to share their origin story, but our whole talk today is going to be about the journey of where you came from and the experiences you had, so it's like one gigantic origin story question. In light of that, I think a great place for us to begin today is with a bit of your early backstory. Tell us about your family, church experience, and other moments from your upbringing that will help to set the stage.

IVAN: Sure, Shaun. As a little kid I grew up in a house where I had a mother who was a great Christian woman. I had a father who walked the fence quite a bit. I grew up loving God. I couldn't wait to get to Sunday school on Sundays. And then when I became a teenager, I was able to go to the youth group on Friday nights. To me, that was the most exciting thing. I loved God. I loved Jesus. I loved all the stories in the Bible. My whole desire was to become a pastor one day of a church and do that. I just thought that'd be the greatest thing on earth.

When I was eight, I got saved and was baptized. When I was ten, I was filled with the Holy Spirit. My whole life completely changed. It's kind of hard to explain, but once you get that done and you just get filled with the Holy Spirit, I would go to youth camp and I'd be wiped out at youth camp. It was in West Virginia where the youth camp used to be for Assemblies of God back then. They would literally have to pick me up off of the floor and carry me to my bunk, put me in it because I would be just out in the Spirit. I loved it. And then I went to Bible college and I thought, "Man, this is it. I'm going to Bible college. I'm going to do what I want to do." And so that's what I did. I went to Bible college. Now, how would you like me to take it from there?

SHAUN: Next, I'd love for you to share the story of your first experience of preaching. Tell us about that.

IVAN: It was actually the first embarrassing moment of my life preaching. I was up in Maine and there was this older building that I was preaching in and it had a wooden floor, no carpet or anything on it, but it was a platform and the platform was raised about two and a half, three feet up. And it had, oh, I don't know what you want to call it, like little register openings at the bottom of it, where air can flow through it. And I'm up there and I'm trying to preach and I'm tapping my foot all the time. I'm preaching and people come up and say different things, like, "I appreciated the sermon this morning." And finally, some old guy comes up and he says, "Well, it was a good sermon this morning, but could you not tap your foot so much on the next one? It was very distracting." I didn't realize it. It was the first sermon I ever preached.

SHAUN: Well, no matter what we're doing, especially when it comes to public speaking and communicating, we all have to go through those first few that are challenging. I feel like a lot of times if our leg is shaking or our foot is tapping, we don't even realize that there's this nervous energy trying to get out of our body in the moment.

Ivan, let's have you take us next to the point at which your life took what we might call a left turn. You were on a trajectory and a path where it definitely sounds like you felt called into ministry. You had a lot of Holy Spirit experiences throughout your childhood and growing-up years. How did you get off on a different path? You were here and then your path veered off.

IVAN: Well, Shaun, I was such an innocent 19-year-old kid. I was going to Bible college and I came home for Christmas break. And I'm a real, pure, innocent kid and I go to the store. It was called the GEM store way back then. It was a government employee membership store back in the Washington DC area. And I go into the store. And when I get in there, there's this beautiful girl working there. And she just started talking to me and she actually was going to get ready to go on a break. And I'm thinking, "Wow, she's pretty. And she's talking to me, this is great." Never had somebody that pretty started a conversation up with me before. And so we got to talking and we went to this little break area there and sat down and talked. Well, one thing led to another and I didn't go back to Bible college. I took a left turn. I was a young man who thought I was in love and I made a mistake. I mean, it was a huge mistake. And so I just drifted off.

> *I didn't go back to Bible college. I took a left turn. I was a young man who thought I was in love and I made a mistake.*

SHAUN: I talk to my own kids about when we get to an age where we actually have a little bit of wisdom. I think we can all look back on our teenage years and as we're in our twenties, we think we know so much or we think we understand a lot. I'm 42 right now and I feel like I'm to a place now where I have enough life experience and enough knowledge that I have a little bit of wisdom, but boy we sure think we have an awful lot of wisdom and an ability to make good decisions when we're young. I think a lot of the audience can relate to that aspect of your story.

Let's fast forward now into 1978, which is the year I was born, actually. You're 26, working at a car dealership, and it sounds like you were doing fairly well in terms of sales. Then all of a sudden you get this strange pain in your leg that you're trying to avoid, but it just won't go away.

IVAN: Let's add a little bit more to that straight away. It was a gradual thing, but by the time I turned 21, I started drinking and started smoking pot. And then I found out what crystal meth was like, what cocaine was like, and when I tell you I took a wrong path, I just did. Now I was working. I was doing great at my job. I was making six figures back in the seventies, and I was selling cars and I was doing it legitimately, having fun with customers. They didn't have to worry about the customer coming back, getting upset. There were new cars, mostly, that I sold and I loved it. I was doing great. You know, I'd probably make about $117,000 a year or something around there. And I was probably making that much more on the side on the drugs, to be blunt with you.

I was into dancing, I was into doing these things. Then all of a sudden my left calf started swelling up on me. I thought, "Man, this is a bad Charlie horse." I kept thinking it was bad. I went to a doctor finally, and the doctor told me, "Hey," he says, "you've got thrombophlebitis."

Now I'll be blunt with you. When I first heard that word, I thought he said I had a trombone in my legs. I'm like, "Trombone, trombone, what's he talking about?" I'd never heard that word before. He started telling me what a blood clot is. And I'm like, I don't have blood clots. I'm 26. My grandfather has blood clots. That's what old people get. You always hear about it. You know? And I just got up off of the table and left his office and thought, "Well, whatever."

He kept telling me, "Hey, listen, it's serious." And I'm like, yeah right. So I left. It wasn't too long after that, a few days later, within a week or so I was in the hospital because my leg was so swollen. The calf of my leg was about the size of the thigh of my leg. It was turning colors and my foot was purple. I couldn't dance anymore, and that was my big thing back then. I used to really dance a lot. At least I thought I could dance well. Do you remember those platform shoes?

SHAUN: I've never worn any, but I do know what you're talking about.

IVAN: Oh dude. I was in good shape back then. I wore the platform shoes, the big heel, the big bellbottom pants, shirts that button all the way down to wherever, big puffy sleeves. And you know, the vest that you can take off and throw—all that stuff. But anyway, getting back to the leg, the leg was swelled up, so I went to the emergency room and they started to examine me and the doctor went away and he said, "Do not move."

And I said, "What do you mean?"

He said, "Don't put your leg down off the side of the bed. Don't do anything. Mister, you've got one of the worst legs I've ever seen for a blood clot." He told me what they were going to do. They were going to just double-check.

> *"Mister, you've got one of the worst legs I've ever seen for a blood clot."*

While they were talking to me, I explained to them that I'm highly allergic to the IVP dye. It was an iodine dye. Because I had that when I was 12 for a kidney problem and almost died. They said if I ever had that, it could kill me. So they did something, I'm the first person in the country they tried it on. They did a radioactive retrograde uptake. Fancy word. What they did was they injected this radioactive material into me, and then they put a Geiger counter over the top of me. That's the best way I can explain it. You lie on this bed and there's this big round thing over you, and it shows this pattern up on this screen and you see all these little dots going all over the place.

Well, the dots weren't going through that leg very well at all. So they said, "Yep. It's definitely a blood clot. It's really bad. Don't move." They put me in the hospital. They kept me in the hospital for around ten days, roughly, and I couldn't move. When I say move, I learned what a bedpan was. And I learned when they tell you that you can't get out of bed, you can't get out of it. You can't even sit up very much. They want you to lie back down, watch TV from a prone position as much as possible. They want you still. So I did everything they told me to do. And then I was released. When I got released, I went home.

Now, you know, I was a single guy back then. I don't know about any other guys out there, but I was looking for sympathy and I wanted somebody to come over and cook something for me. So I called this girl up and she came over. I got home around five o'clock. She picked me up something to eat. The first thing I had to do was smoke a joint. And she brought some beer, which I don't like beer, but I drank a beer and smoked some more pot.

IVAN TUTTLE DIED AND ENCOUNTERED SATAN IN HELL BEFORE SEEING GOD IN HEAVEN

Even to this day, I'm usually still up until 2, 3, 4 a.m., it just depends. It was nine o'clock and I'm like, "You know, something's wrong. I feel really tired. I feel really sleepy." And I told the girl, I said, "Hey, you know, just sit out here and watch TV a little bit or do whatever. I've got to go lay down. Something's wrong." I went into my bedroom and I lay down on my free flotation water bed. I had one of those. I loved that thing. I wish they still made them.

I was sleeping on my left side; I always liked to sleep on my left side, because I had something called hypertrophic cardiomyopathy at the time. When you have hypertrophic cardiomyopathy, if you sleep on your left side, it helps the heart to be better. And so I lay down and I was sleeping on my left side and I fell asleep. I mean, I fell asleep fast. All of a sudden, something grabbed a hold of my left wrist and yanked me straight up out of the bed. And when I say yanked me, I mean, this thing grabbed a hold of me.

Now, as I told you, I was in good shape back then. I was one of these people that if I ever had to defend myself, it was usually one punch and it was over. I was very strong and I hit this thing as hard as I could. It had zero effect on it. And it just looked at me. It was the most demonic-looking thing. And I was like, "Wait a minute. What's going on?" And I turned around, you know, and looked at my bed like, "How did you get me out of the bed? I'm still in bed. Wait a minute. Oh." And then I'm thinking, "This is a bad dream, a bad nightmare." I went to turn on the light switch and my hand went right through the wall and the light switch didn't work. And then I knew I was dead.

I went to turn on the light switch and my hand went right through the wall and the light switch didn't work. And then I knew I was dead.

It's kind of hard to explain, but it's like your spirit wakes up and your spirit goes, "Buddy, you're dead. I'm out of your body now. I can start doing the thinking instead of your brain doing it. Let me tell you what's going on." And I was looking at this thing and realizing this thing is taking me to hell. I knew it. I knew what was going to go on. I knew I was going to hell and next thing you know, we're going.

This demon has me. And I'm hearing all these screams. I'm hearing people yelling, you know, people screaming. It's pitch black there, but in the spirit you can see through that blackness and you can see the people. And here's the remarkable thing. When you see people, when you're in the spirit only, you see people instantly. When you look at them, you know absolutely everything about their life. You know every little detail in their life, every little thing that goes on in their life; there's not a thing that you don't know.

As I looked at these people, so many were wondering, "Why am I in hell? What am I doing here? What did I do wrong? Get me outta here. I need to get out of here somehow." But they all knew, even those who were Christians at one time in their life, they knew that they were in hell. All their prayers, when they try to pray from hell, it's like an iron dome is over it. They're not going anywhere. It's like it just hits something and it stops. And these people were screaming. The smell, the stench was horrible.

These people were screaming. The smell, the stench was horrible.

Now I never saw flames, but I felt this intense heat all the time. It was an intense heat. These demons would sit there and I'd watch them with other people. They did the same thing to me. They stab you with things. They pull on you. They jerk on you. They stick you with great big, long thorns or something. They stick them into you. It's the most horrible feeling. On earth, when you get a splinter, you know that that little dinky splinter hurts so bad in that finger. Can you imagine that same pain from a little splinter through your whole body? That's what it's like—your whole being, your whole spirit being, it feels every ounce of the pain. So intense. But the difference is when you're in the flesh, you can pass out. In the spirit, you live with that pain. And here's the thing to remember—that pain lasts forever. It never stops. It keeps going and going. Listen, a hundred million years, we can think, "Okay, a hundred million years," our mind can kind of grasp that. But a hundred million years isn't even a tenth of a second in eternity. It's like nothing.

I think the thing that was the worst of all was knowing there's no hope. When you are in hell, all those people in there, they know there's no hope. I mean, they want to get out, but they know it's over. It's over, man. Once that happens, there's no getting out of it. You know, I'm one in like 500 billion. I don't know if there's anybody else that's ever gone through what I went through. I just know that when I was in hell, I knew this was it. It was final. And I didn't think I was ever going to get out of this. It was the most horrible, horrible feeling. Even when I talk about it today, my eyes are tearing up. I'm trying not to, here, but my eyes tear up because of the hopelessness that you feel, the horrible feeling that you have because the pain is so intense, the smell is so gross, and it never stops.

***I just know that when I was in hell,
I knew this was it. It was final.***

Shaun, it's like it penetrates all of your being. The smell just comes through you and it's so gross. And in the laughter of them laughing at you—you're not laughing, but the demons are laughing. They're making fun of you. You fell for it, buddy. You're the stupid idiot who didn't listen to God. You're the one who turned your back on Him, especially people who have been Christians. The demons love it.

Now, listen, I even saw pastors in hell, former pastors, former evangelists who were in there. Now I'm not going to name names. God will not allow me. He won't release me to do that for various reasons. But I can tell you that some of them were people we knew, famous people, but they're in hell for various reasons. Some because they did things they shouldn't have done sexually with children and with other adults and things. There are some there because they stole and robbed people. I mean, literally, there are some there because they were very vicious toward their family, and these are people who never asked for forgiveness. They justified what they did. They tried to justify it and say, "Hey, it's okay. God still loves me. I still have my anointing, so it's still okay that I'm doing this." No, it's not. I saw that, and that's what took me into hell.

SHAUN: I've read quite a few books about near-death experiences, heaven encounters, and hell encounters. Ivan, yours is the first that I've encountered where you talk about the demon pulling you into the center of the pit of hell, if you will, where you encountered the devil or satan, which is this angel of light and beauty. I thought that was kind of striking because it fits with what we read in scripture and what we see talked about throughout church history. So I would love to have you just comment on that briefly. I felt like that actually gave an extra level of credibility to what you're sharing in your story.

IVAN: Sure. This is the thing, satan or lucifer, he's not this big scary guy with horns popping out of his head and a long tail. That's something that his demons helped create in order to put fear into people. What lucifer or satan looks like, he is probably the most beautiful creature you've ever seen on earth. He is so handsome and so good-looking and so beautiful. And there's this light that still emits from him. He hasn't lost that, that light still emits from him. Let me tell you what, he could talk anybody into doing anything. He has a lot of power—as long as you don't have Christ in you, he's got a lot of power. And when he comes around, if you're important enough for him to come around, that's a really powerful thing because his beauty is second to none. You've never seen it. Even men will sit there and look at him and go, "Wow, I wish I looked like that," because it's just how you would feel. And even when I was in hell, I'm thinking, wow. You know, if I had a look like that, I would have had the world by the tail, so to speak. Those are the thoughts that run through your head, even when you're in hell and you're seeing it. So I see him for who he is.

SHAUN: So Ivan, you're in hell. And all of a sudden, you hear this thunderous voice. You're in this hopeless place and then all of a sudden there's a breakthrough and a shift happens. Take us into that part of your story.

IVAN: Yes. This demon was taking me and putting me in my final place. What I mean by your final place is when you go to hell, you're put in a place that you're going to be in forever. You're not moving around. You're not walking around. You're not partying down there. Get that out of your head. That shouldn't be a part of your speech anyway. But you know, people say, "Oh, I'm going to party down there, dude." That's not a party. It's almost like there's a chain, but you don't see it. There's a chain around your waist and you get put in your final place. Your feet move around, but you don't go anywhere. Your feet just kind of dangle and you can move your arms around, but you're locked in a place as these demons start in. And this demon was getting ready to put me in my final place.

As he was doing that, a voice rang out and this voice said, "It's not his time. I made a promise to his mother. You must let him go." This voice was so powerful that this demon, which I was still trying to fight with, this demon was hitting me and he was poking me and stabbing me. All of a sudden he cowered down. He was like, "Oh no!" and he let go of me. Thank God. And instantly I was translated right to the gates of heaven. And there I was greeted by this great big angel. Now this angel could be seven or eight feet tall. I didn't go around with a measuring stick, but I can just tell you he was tall. I had to really look up at him. He was tall and he was a good-looking guy. He had this powerful, gentle voice when he'd speak.

A voice rang out and this voice said, "It's not his time. I made a promise to his mother. You must let him go."

It's kind of hard to explain how we communicated, but you could hear his voice. It kind of just went through you and you knew it was an angel. And he said, "Hey, you need to take my hand. You're not ready for this. You're going to have to go back to earth and straighten out your life, but God wants me to show you some things." So he took me by the hand and he brought me into the gates of heaven. And we walked into the gates of heaven.

SHAUN: Ivan, one thing I'd like to have you do before we get into more of your heaven encounter is contrast the difference in what was hitting your senses. You talked about how in hell, the intensity of everything hitting your spiritual senses was just off the charts. Talk to us about what was hitting your senses in heaven.

IVAN: One word describes it. Euphoric. You go from total desolation, no hope, no anything. You're, you're so burdened and heavy that all of a sudden now you're, "Oh yes, oh man." You know, you feel everything. You feel the glory of God going through you. It tingles everything that you have, all your senses are tingling. And it's like, oh, you can taste it. You can feel it. And all that smell that was on you is gone and it smells beautiful there. You smell good up there. Your senses are so heightened, even more so than ever. Even the spiritual senses that you have become so great because now you can look at something and instantly know everything. You can look at Google and you can outperform Google. If somebody was typing something in, you could answer it before they even finish asking the question. That's where you get to when you're in the spirit, especially when the glory of God is all over you, because that's what happens when you go into heaven—His glory is over you. There's nothing like it.

When you go into heaven—His glory is over you. There's nothing like it.

IVAN TUTTLE DIED AND ENCOUNTERED SATAN IN HELL BEFORE SEEING GOD IN HEAVEN

SHAUN: Ivan, take us back to where we were just a moment ago. The angel took your hand and led you through the gates. Tell us what happened next.

IVAN: The first thing I saw was a huge city and these huge white buildings, I've never seen. It was like white marble stone that sparkled. And it was just gloriously white. I can only think it was like a marble, but it looked like it was studded with diamonds through it. It was just glorious and beautiful. I saw lots of trees, mountains, everything, but I saw these two big trees by the river that ran right down to the city, right down the middle of the street. Now this river was beautiful. It was crystal clear. In fact, you look at it and you're like, "Is there really water in there?" It was so clear. But then it got to an area where it was bubbling and it sounded like little babies laughing. Have you ever heard little babies laughing when they think something is really funny? It almost sounded like that. And I watched that.

Then there were streets that looked like gold, but it was soft when you stepped on it. And it was like, "Oh, this is amazing." You can step on it and move around and do things. And it's really an amazing feeling that you get when you do that. And it's so beautiful. And you look at the trees, now—there were 12 different fruits to come out on this tree. And they come out at different times and you can see it. And sometimes God will say, "Hey, let Me show you this." Boom, boom, boom. All 12 different fruits will come out. That was the experience I was allowed to see at the time. And it was very, very unique. So that's just some of what I saw.

SHAUN: I've got more questions about heaven, so we'll keep going. You share a little bit about seeing people being greeted by friends and family when they entered heaven. Talk to us about what you saw there.

IVAN: I didn't put this in the book, but I need to tell you a little something here. One of the things that I did see was I had a sister who was stillborn and I got to see her. She was there in heaven. I got to see my great-grandfather on my father's side. He was in heaven. I had no idea, you know, that he was a Christian. He was a strong Christian man. He was in heaven. I got to see other people.

Now here's the remarkable thing. If you don't mind me getting into this, it has to do with little babies. Would you mind? Here's the thing that I saw—I saw all the aborted babies in heaven, waiting. They're in an area waiting for their mothers to show up. They're waiting for their fathers to show up. They're waiting because every single one of them is in heaven. There isn't a single one who didn't make it into heaven. And they're waiting.

We know that people make mistakes in their life. And if they just ask God to forgive them for their mistakes, just like with me, when they get to heaven they get to see their little ones. And God does this strange thing and I haven't talked about this much before, but God does this thing. If that parent needs to see what it's like to have that little baby, God allows that child to become a little baby so they can hold it, just to see what that's like. And then He lets the baby kind of grow up real quick, but God allows that to happen so that the parent can get that feeling that they didn't get, that they lost.

That to me was still the most lasting thing in my mind. Everything was beautiful and great, but seeing those little babies. Miscarried babies, stillborn babies, or children who died at a very young age—they're there. They're waiting. When you see a mother who was going through something in her life and she did something wrong that she thought, oh no, and then she's reunited with her child and that child greets her. Oh man, that's so powerful!

Miscarried babies, stillborn babies, or children who died at a very young age—they're there. They're waiting.

SHAUN: It's hard to think of a more exciting reunion than a mother and a father reuniting with their lost child. I love that God allowed you to see that. Another part of the book that really struck me was where you talked about music in heaven. Tell us what you experienced with music. I think you said something to the effect of it's like it goes through your body.

IVAN: Oh, it does. I'm going to let you know something—here's a secret from heaven. When music is played, it ignites the spirit and activates the spirit before the flesh ever hears it, because the spirit is more in tune. Music came from heaven. Music wasn't something that we invented on earth. Music came from heaven. So music was made for the spirit, not for the flesh. So be careful what you listen to. Music in heaven, when it hits you, it penetrates your body. You taste it. It's like, mm, that tastes good.

You feel the music. You see the music. You hear the music. It goes through you and you can feel the melodies. You can feel the different things, the notes. I mean, literally you feel like you want to rise on something and your spirit is doing it. Your spirit reacts to it. And oh, there's nothing like it. And when you hear them singing holy, holy, holy—oh, it's so deep. Everything inside of you is like, yes, holy, worshiping God. Oh, I'm a lover of music now, way beyond those people. I'm not musically talented. I can carry a tune, but I don't have the best tone in the world to sing. I can sing "This Little Light of Mine," I can do good on that. Other than that, I'm kind of out of it. But you know, I love to sing.

This past week I happened to be around some very musical people. I was listening. I was like, oh, I was just lost in it. The music in heaven. When you understand what it does to your spirit, listen, folks. If you're having problems at home, put worship music on. I'm going to be blunt—I'm not talking about rap music. Okay? Worship music. I'm talking about worship music that is pleasant to the ears and pleasant to the spirit and the soul. Nothing's wrong with the Christian rap music. It's for a generation, but you want to have something you can soak in the Word of God and just let it soak into you. You turn that on. You know what? Demons hate it.

This is what I saw from heaven. The demons hate it when you have worship music. Why, when they start worshiping in church and they start doing the music, they should just let the music go for a lot longer because the demons are like, "Ah, I can't stand it!" They're covering up their ears. They can't handle it because it's not worshiping lucifer. It's worshiping God. It's giving praises to Jesus, giving praises to God. It's not giving praises to lucifer. So they hate it. The worldly music—every kind of worldly music, I don't care what it is—it's not worshiping God, even though God gave them that talent to do what they do. Unfortunately, they use it for the wrong reason. And so that activates another thing in your spirit. So just think about that. Music is awesome. Do you know that people with Alzheimer's, if you play music, they can sing a song when they can't even talk to somebody? But you play music, they can sing a song. Where does that come from?

SHAUN: Music is very powerful. I think in a sense it transcends the mind and it can flow right in. So that's where messaging and music are really important. Because we're kind of bypassing our logic and just taking it right in. And in terms of people who are gifted with musical talents, if it's not to create, give praise and worship to the Lord, it's really just to bring praise and worship to another kingdom.

Next, Ivan, I'd love to have you talk about angels. You talked about encountering different types of angels in heaven. In the same sense, you talked earlier about being in the spirit. Did you just intuitively know what kind of angels they were or what their purpose was? I'm curious how that worked out, because, you know, in terms of different kinds of angels in the Bible, it's not always as specific as we'd like it to be. So I'm curious how you came to understand what sorts of angels they were and what their purpose was.

IVAN: Well, I was told what they were. I cheated. I paid attention for once. You know there's a power that angels carry, and the most powerful angels are archangels. When you're in their presence, it's almost like being in the presence of God—it's that strong. It's that powerful. When an archangel appears, do not mess with it because they're going to appear for something that's really special.

When an archangel appears, do not mess with it because they're going to appear for something that's really special.

There are angels that have wings; there are angels that don't have wings. There are angels that look like you and me, and to prove a point, I don't have the passage in front of me right now but it's in Acts. If you remember, when Peter got out of prison, he went up and he knocked on the outer door and the girl ran and said, "Oh, I forgot to unlock the door." She said, "Oh, it's Peter," and ran back in to everybody, and they said, "No, it must be his angel." Well, why did they say that? Because there are angels that can look just like you and appear someplace where you might not be.

Sometimes you hear people say, "Oh, somebody was in someplace." I've had people tell me before, like I'm up in the state of Washington and somebody in Florida says, "Hey, I saw you today. You talked to me."

And I'm like, "Really?"

"Yeah, I was talking to you about your book."

And I'm like, "Okay, where?"

"Down here in Florida."

And I'm going, no, I wasn't there. So as far as I know, that's one of my angels. That's all I know. And so those things happen. There are messenger angels, there are angels that are dispatched to bring you a message that are coming. You'll have angels that can appear in the middle of the night or just be standing next to you and constantly talking to you in your ear. Hopefully you can hear them. Your spirit hears them, but you have to get your mind in tune to it by allowing the spirit.

Here's the key to listening to God and listening to things that God wants you to hear—you have to allow your spirit to rule your brain, not your brain rule your spirit. We've been taught through religion that our brain must control our spirit. The reality is our spirit must control the brain because that's the way it was designed. We were designed so that when God breathed into the nostrils of Adam, it was to activate his spirit so that he can keep his mind going. We need to learn to do that.

You have a guardian angel. You really do have one. There's one there. Some people can see angels and some people can't. I can't tell you why, but these angels have different assignments. Angels are coming to bring you things. You've heard of people getting in a wreck, about ready to hit a cement truck, and all of a sudden their car veers off to the right and they never turned the steering wheel. Well, that's your guardian angel that did that. People can say what they want, but they're real.

SHAUN: Ivan, I'd love to hear next about things that you were shown in heaven. Did you encounter things about the future or potentially your future assignment? Obviously, you were there and it was a fantastic experience, but you did end up coming back here to earth with an assignment. So what sorts of other things were you shown while you were in heaven?

IVAN: Oh, it was a real disappointment to come back.

SHAUN: I hear that from a lot of people who've been to heaven, where it pained them to have to leave heaven and come back to earth.

IVAN: If I had stayed dead, I'd be in hell. I wouldn't have been able to stay in heaven. God brought me up there to send me back with a message.

Now you have to remember who was in office in the United States of America in 2013, when I started writing out these things. We were in such a far-left world. And God said our next president is going to be a different president. He's going to be a conservative president. And God let me see that in 2013. And so that's one of the things that I saw about the future. Well, I saw it in 1978, but I wrote about it in 2013. He said, "I want you to write this; now is the time for it to happen." And I'm thinking I'm going to be locked up for writing this.

Nope, this is what happened. I saw earthquakes. I saw, for instance, holes opening up in Russia—unusual type holes, great big holes. It looked like somebody took a big drill and just drilled into the ground. And some were 200 feet across or better. And they were huge. It was up in Siberia, Russia. Did you know that place is called "the end of the world"? That's what the locals call it. Now that just seems to be strange, you know? It's in the book too, because it's what God said. It was really funny because when God said, "Write about that," I was like, "Okay, Lord, I don't know why."

He said, "Because I'm going to do some confirmations on it."

So that's just some of the things. I saw things happening in China. I saw rivers turning red overnight. And since I wrote that, rivers are starting to turn red overnight. I saw future things coming. There are futuristic things that are coming. When I say buildings and space, they're going to be putting more people out there. We're talking about space stations, but almost like buildings out there. There's going to be so much junk that we put into space. And we think that we can do that. And that's going to be a holding platform because they want to send people to other places and other planets. And they're going to start building more things and doing more. And that's their thoughts. That's their thought process of doing things. I watched what was going to happen on earth.

I watched a new device that's coming out and it's going to be planted inside of our ear. You need to recharge it eventually, but it runs off of the energy from your body because our bodies put off energy. We actually put out an electric pattern that comes off of us and that'll stay in your ear. It's almost invisible. You can hardly see it and you can use it connected to your phone. You can make phone calls, you can do different things. You know, these are just different things that I saw. I saw so many different things about the future. You know, the future climate I saw what's going to happen in Russia. I saw what's going to happen in China. I saw what's going to happen in Africa, in South America, Australia, and New Zealand.

There are earthquakes that are coming. There are things that are coming, but don't think it's all doom and gloom. There is a glory that's coming. Brother, there's a glory coming that's going to be so strong, people are going to have what I call the Peter anointing. When they walk down the street, their shadow will land on somebody and that person will be healed. That person might not even be a believer or know anything about it, but the shadow will hit them and all of a sudden, if they can't walk, they get up and start walking. Or if they had cancer, all of a sudden, "Oh, I'm breathing well. What's going on?" Their cancer is cured. They have Type 2 diabetes or Type 1 diabetes—boom, it's healed. This is going to start happening. This is a greater glory that's going to happen. I saw it happen. It's coming and it's going to be huge. It's going to be there, not just for a few months, not just for a couple of years, but for a long time. And it's coming. It's very shortly coming.

This is a greater glory that's going to happen. I saw it happen. It's coming and it's going to be huge.

SHAUN: Wow. Well, I guess all I can say to that is amen. It's amazing to think that the presence that people are going to carry is so strong that it is going to be like that Peter anointing, when the presence even in your shadow is so strong that sickness and evil cannot remain in that space because it has been filled with the glory and goodness of God. Wow. That's a fantastic concept to think of. I love that.

Ivan, I often find with people who've had heaven experiences, God will often give them special gifts or abilities. Were there any specific gifts that God gave you that would relate to your assignment when you went back to earth?

IVAN: Yeah, but if I tell you, you won't talk to me anymore.

SHAUN: I talk to prophetic people all the time, so I always wonder when they won't call me back or email me, I'm like, "Gosh, are they seeing bad things about me in the spirit?"

IVAN: Would you like to know? It's all good, brother. It's one of the things that God gave me. People think it's crazy, but He gave me a gift to be able, if I look at a person's eyes, even if I look at a picture of somebody, the Lord just reveals everything about this person to me. Now that doesn't mean I'm allowed to tell you everything, but here's what happens—I'll look at someone and I know things.

One time my son and I were pulling into a parts department store to get a part for a car. There was this white truck that was starting to back out of a spot. I looked over there, and I just instantly blurted it out. And I said, "This guy is a bank robber."

My son thought I was crazy. He's going, "Right, Dad?"

And I said, "No, he's a bank robber." So I wrote his tag number down and went to a payphone by a Target. I picked up the payphone with some paper towels on it because I didn't want anybody to find out it was me and think I was a nut. So I dialed 911 and I said, "Hey, listen, here's the license plate number to the guy who's been robbing these banks. You might want to check it out. It's a white Ford truck." And I hung up the phone and I drove away from there. I made sure there were no cameras. Right? I put a hat on my head and everything else like that, parked the car around the back of the building. I didn't want anybody to say, "Hey, who's this guy? Call him in."

About two weeks later, they arrested the guy driving a white Ford pickup truck. He had been robbing banks. So I mean, that's the kind of thing it is. Then also, until he was age 18, God allowed me to see my son wherever he was, every place. So this is a story you don't know about. I'll make it quick. When he got old enough, you know, my son would be driving down the road. "Okay, Dad, where am I?"

And I go, "Well, this is where you're at."

He goes, "Okay, Dad, where are you?" And I'm at work or I'm at home. And he goes, "Come on, Dad, how do you know that's where I'm at?"

I said, "I see you." And I kept telling him this. We lived up in Northern Idaho, and my son drove an old winter beater car. It was his first big car he was going to drive on his own to school. He needed something like that, a big boat. The headliner kept falling down; something was wrong with it. The dash was shaking too.

Well, one day when he turned 21, he decided to come tell me what he did when he was 17. I had told him the headliner kept falling down, and he goes, "Yeah, Dad, I know." He finally told me that one day after football practice, he and his buddies had gone out there and torn the whole car apart. They took the headlights out and looked back behind the dash. They took the dashboard apart, looked up underneath it, pulled wires down that never got connected again, took the headliner down. They took it apart looking for cameras and microphones. And he said, "You know, Dad, after we couldn't find anything, that made me realize God really did show you." So that's just him.

God also allowed me to pray for people and they get healed. It's not because of anything I do. I just obey what's supposed to be done. It's like being a lightning rod—when the lightning hits, the lightning goes down through it and that's it. So those things happen. But God allows me to see things. There are just so many different gifts. There's a lot of other things, things that I can't even talk about yet.

I just obey what's supposed to be done. It's like being a lightning rod— when the lightning hits, the lightning goes down through it and that's it.

SHAUN: I like that analogy of the lightning rod, because you are like a conduit God's power flows through for these things to happen. It's been really interesting, as somebody who came out of a more conservative church space. Because God has a sense of humor, eight years ago I got thrown into the deep end of the charismatic world, and now this is my home. But just to see the intersection of charismatic, prophetic culture in mainstream secular culture right now. I know prophetic people who are speaking into kidnapping situations and cases like that. People who are prophetic are speaking into business and all the places that prophetic influences are coming to a head in these days. It's very different than what you saw five to ten years ago. I'm very fascinated to see the trajectory God has His church on as He gives us opportunities to speak in more spheres of culture that we wouldn't have necessarily even had influence in before, yet God in His sovereignty is opening those doors.

Well, Ivan let's get to the tail end of your hell and heaven encounter. You're sent back. In fact, you are thrust back into your body. Tell us about leaving heaven and waking up in your bedroom.

IVAN: Well, it was very disappointing. Here's what I saw. I watched as I was kicked out of heaven. Talk about rejection, but I had to go back and I knew I had to go back so I can go back to heaven for good. And I knew I was on a mission when I got back. So I was coming back into my body and I was in the room seeing these two paramedics—one kind of tall, thin guy, and then another shorter, stockier man. The shorter, stockier man had already come over and checked me. He turned around and looked at the other guy and he was shaking his head, "No, man, this guy's dead." The blood was starting to coagulate in my wrist and in my elbow. When he went to move it just a little bit, it wasn't real stiff, but it was stiffening up. Rigor mortis was already beginning to set in just a little bit, and I was dead. I was so far gone, they just walked out of the room. They were calling the morgue, and the radio wouldn't work in that apartment. So he went to use my phone and the taller guy said, "Hey, there's a girl in the apartment so you might want to just kind of check him to make sure he's not bleeding someplace, that she hasn't committed some crime or something."

So he came walking back in there and he went to put his hand down underneath my side to just check to see if there was any blood any place. When that happened, I came back to life. I came into my body. Well, when I came into my body, I couldn't breathe. My whole body started vibrating like it got shocked with 240 volts and I couldn't talk. And this guy jumped back. I keep joking and say I scared him to death and he scared me to life.

But he kind of jumped back and he was just kind of looking at me, you know? And I was trying to talk, and my jaws didn't want to work. My tongue was not working. My eyes were real dry, because my eyes were open. It was just a weird feeling. And nothing wanted to work right. For quite a little while, you know, I was trying to talk and to say things and to breathe. They were trying to say, "We need to take you to a hospital." No. That was the first word I could get out was *no, no, no*. I was trying to move and I couldn't really move. Finally, I struggled with it and they got me up out of the bed.

IVAN TUTTLE DIED AND ENCOUNTERED SATAN IN HELL BEFORE SEEING GOD IN HEAVEN

I told him, "I need to stand up, need to stand up," and they're trying to check me; they're putting a blood pressure thing on me. They're trying to do whatever they can and I'm going, "No, no." I could say "no." Then I was saying, "Leave, leave, leave." I could get the word *leave* out. Finally, I just told him to get out of there—I started being able to speak. Not clearly. It was weird. Even my voice sounded strange and it was kind of hoarse sounding. And I got them over to the front door. I walked enough to get there, but it was a shaky walk. Believe me, it was a weird walk because my bones were all stiffened up or something. They didn't move correctly. My brain was telling them to move, but my legs were like, "I ain't moving." Finally, they started moving.

So everything started working again just right, and they left. I kicked the girl out too. I grabbed her purse and her jacket and gave it to her and she left. It was cold out there. I wasn't going to make her leave without her jacket. And so everybody left. I have to be honest with you. I had a lot of drugs in my apartment and the cocaine was easy to flush, but marijuana does not flush. When you put it in the commode, you have to put tons of toilet paper on it and wet it, because it just won't go down. So I was trying to get rid of all of this stuff because I wanted nothing to do with it. I knew that I was never going to go back to that lifestyle.

So after I got rid of the drugs, I dumped the booze I had there—I had a little bit of alcohol there in the house and the beer that she brought over, and I dumped all that down the kitchen sink. I had an avocado green rocking chair from the seventies. You're too young to probably remember those, but I had one of those and it was a low back and it didn't have a real high back on it, you know? That thing would rock back and forth and swivel around. I sat in that thing and I rocked and I cried. Brother, I cried so hard because I had a second chance. I wasn't going to stay in hell, I had a second chance, and I was thinking of all these things and just crying out to God, "Forgive me, God, forgive me, forgive me."

How could I have been so foolish? How could I have been so stupid? I mean, I'm being blunt, but to me, that's stupid and so foolish to just walk away from God. And I cried and wept and I sat in that rocking chair for hours. I cried until 6:30 in the morning, and this was around midnight when it started, a little after midnight. I cried. I mean, I went through a whole box of Kleenex.

It's something when you go through that experience. And the angel said I can't talk about it. Now, I could say that I died. And I could say I went to hell and I went to heaven, and I could say a little bit about how I saw some things in hell. I didn't go into detail. And I saw some things in heaven that I was released and allowed to go to heaven. So I went to the hospital to tell the doctor because it was important—I had to know whether I was going crazy or what.

The doctor sat there and I told him. I'll never forget. He sat up in his chair. He had an office in there. It was about the size of a closet. And he sat forward and leaned in and he looked at me and he said, "Listen, I believe that what you went through was real.

I'm not saying that I think *you* think it was real. I believe that what you went through was real. I've had patients tell me they went to hell. I've had patients tell me they went to heaven, but you're the first one who went to both." So he said I had a real experience. And he said most of them were only dead for a few seconds, but I had been dead for about three hours, they estimated. And he said, "Yeah, you went there. There's no explanation."

Now, can I bring one other thing up that happened to me? There was a miracle that happened to me. I had something called hypertrophic cardiomyopathy. Hypertrophic cardiomyopathy is something that you cannot get rid of without a heart transplant. You have to have a heart transplant to get rid of it. There's no other way to get rid of it. It's a thickening of the muscles of the heart, because your heart is nothing but a big muscle. And the walls of the heart are thick, especially on the left side, and it's hereditary.

My father died at 56. My oldest sister died at 56. I have a sister who is 71 right now. She has it. I have a brother who's in his fifties. He has it real bad, and all their children have it. The grandchildren have it. Everybody's got it. It doesn't skip a generation. It doesn't skip a person. I had it. Everything was set up there. We had some blood drawn from way back when, and there was a genetic marker for it. I had it, I had been tested for it. I had it. I don't have it. God took care of that. It's gone. It was a generational curse. It was broken. I don't have it anymore. I mean, I really don't. I just had another exam. In fact, I gave it to Sid Roth and I said, "Here here's my exam. I don't have it, it's gone."

My sister, Carolyn—her last name is Biro—she started the first cardiomyopathy foundation and you can probably look her up online. You can see Carolyn Biro. Of course, she died, but she still had that. That's still going on. She started that up and she educated doctors on it. So that'll just give you an idea. God healed me through all of that. Instead of coming back and having my heart, my lungs, my kidneys damaged—and my brain might be damaged—but all these things should have been damaged beyond repair. God fixed my heart. He gave me a new one.

---

*God fixed my heart.
He gave me a new one.*

SHAUN: Thank you for sharing that, Ivan. I'm curious to hear, when it was time to begin talking about, writing about your experience, how did you know? How did God say, "Hey, Ivan, it is time to start moving forward with this"?

IVAN: Well, after 35 years, I was getting a little discouraged. After seven years, I kind of quit asking Him, because I'd be like, "Okay, Lord, now can I?" and He'd be like "Not yet. Not yet, soon." And I'm thinking, "Oh, well, His *soon* and my *soon* are like two different things." I've learned that. And then finally, it was August 17, 2013, and it's just like a voice spoke to me and said, "I want you to write a book. I want you to write your testimony now. You're going to write a book." Now, I don't know if anybody else out there has ever heard of ADHD.

SHAUN: A few of us have, I think.

IVAN: I am a perfect candidate. I've been diagnosed with that for many years. Of course, back when I was diagnosed it was just diagnosed with "you're a bad kid." Back in the fifties, they had no idea what that was. So in the fifties and sixties, nobody had ever heard of it hardly at all, but that's what I have. And it was amazing because I'm thinking, "Okay, God, now don't get me wrong. I can write a TV commercial." Cause that's, you know, 30, 60 seconds. And I can have a lot of fun with that. But you know, when you have to write a book, I'm like, "God, I don't know what to do." And He said, "Just sit down."

So I pulled up my laptop. I sat down on the end of the sofa, and I started typing and I thought an hour went by. I had eight pages. Okay. Now I've never typed eight pages in my life. And I had eight pages typed out. I was so proud of myself. I thought, "Well, there we go. There's my testimony." You know? And I printed it off and I thought, "Wow, man, this is good. I got my testimony." And of course I gave it to a few people and everybody's going, "Well, where's the details on this?"

"What do you mean?"

"Well, there's no details in it."

"I know, but look at what happened! I'm alive and God did this." And they still wanted the details. So I took those eight pages and I just sat there and I said, "God, what's going on here?"

And He said, "That's your outline. Start writing, just take the first part that you have and just add to it."

And I'm like, "Well, God, I don't know how to write a book."

He says, "Don't worry. I know the author of the best-selling book in the world. It's called the Bible. I'll help you."

So that's how it happened. And it was like, ah, I was so relieved to finally talk about it and all this stuff just started flooding my mind.

Now I would never read any books about anybody else dying, going to hell, or going to heaven or anything like that. I didn't want to read anything that anybody else had written because I didn't want to taint my mind. I wanted my experience to be 100 percent mine. People knew what I was writing. They were trying to send me books, "Read this book, read that."

I'm like, "No, this is something between God and me," you know? And so that's how it happened. And it was such a release to have that happen. And then finally in April of 2014, I published the first part of my book. It was good.

SHAUN: As they say, the rest is history.

It's almost time for us to wrap up, Ivan, and I want to have you pray in just a moment. But first, if you had to share a call to action, your plea to every person who encounters our conversation or reads your book—what's that takeaway you want to make sure every person hears from your story?

IVAN: Well, this is what I want them to know. I want them to know heaven is real. They have to understand that, but also they need to understand that hell is real. And if you want to be a Christian, it's not something where you just go and you confess Christ as your Lord and Savior once, and then you go about living your life. Being a Christian means to be Christ-like. So if you're really going to be Christ-like, I mean, you want to be like Christ, you need to change your life. You need to turn your life around. You need to say, "Okay, this is what I need to do. I need to connect with God. I need to make sure that I can be more like Christ, that I can do the things that He did because He asks us to do the things He did and greater."

Well, He wouldn't have asked us or told us that we can do that if He didn't know that we could do that. He didn't just give us that and say, "Here, you can do these things and greater, maybe." There was no *maybe* added to that. They didn't have that word, *maybe*. So it was like, "You can do it, go do it." He said to go do it. That means that we are supposed to do it. And if we really are men and women of God, that's what we're supposed to do. We're children of God. Jesus is our Brother in many respects. You can look at it like that. And you have to understand that you've got to live a life. You can't backslide. Backsliding is real. Anybody that says, "Oh, Jesus will never leave you or forsake you," no, He won't. But you'll walk away from Him.

Why did Jesus always warn you be careful, be careful, be careful, be careful? Because He wanted you to be careful that you didn't get snatched away, that you didn't get taken away, because you can be taken away and, believe me, it's so simple. It's little things that you don't expect. And those little things come along and *boom*. I was a pure, innocent kid, very innocent. The devil knew that pretty girl, she's gonna get him, and she got me. She wasn't an evil person. It wasn't that she came after me from a demonic stance necessarily. But satan knew what I would do if that was put in front of me. Because you know what? He's had thousands of years of practice checking us out, seeing what we do.

Why did Jesus always warn you be careful, be careful, be careful, be careful? Because He wanted you to be careful that you didn't get snatched away.

God is real. This earth was formed. God formed this earth for us. Everything that we have here was made for us. It wasn't made for the animals. It wasn't made for just God to come down and enjoy it. God made us to have dominion over the earth. That's what He gave us, and this whole earth was designed and made just for us to be here. And we need to understand that we need to walk in His glory. We need to turn our lives around. If you consider yourself a man or woman of God, what are you doing? That's the number one thing. What are you doing? If you're not doing something for God, then you're stale. You're lukewarm. You have to wake up. This is the end times. It was the end times when the apostles were alive after Jesus died. It's still the end times. We don't know when that final curtain is going to go.

I'm not trying to scare you. I'm just trying to put sense into you. You don't know. And what your job is—your job is to win as many souls as you can. Your job is also to live a life that you're supposed to live that's like Christ. And if you're not living that life, it's time to repent. There's hidden, intentional sin out there where people are hiding their sins. They're hidden, they're intentional, and they're hiding that sin. They think they can hide it from everybody. They're not hiding it from God. God sees that sin. God knows that you're sinning and God sees it and He's checking up on you and believe me, He's watching everything you do. I want you to understand that God's for real and you need to change your life.

I want you to understand that God's for real and you need to change your life.

SHAUN: I think that was one of the unexpected turns in your book. Your book is really pressing into the danger of those intentional, hidden, secret sins and how they can torpedo our Christian journey. And so Ivan, however you feel led, I'd love for you to close us in prayer.

IVAN: Heavenly Father, we just come before You now, God. Lord, I know You're allowing me to see these people who are out there watching this. God, You're allowing me to see it spiritually. Heavenly Father, I pray for each and every one of them, that God, You'll just reach out and You just take Your hand and You just show them how much You love them. That You'd just scoop them up in Your hand and You put them next to Your chest and You say, "I love you, brother. I love you, sister. I want your life to change. I want you to be more like My other Son, His name's Jesus." Turn your life around right now in Jesus' name. I declare and decree that everybody who reads this, there'll be an awakening that happens inside of you. That you'll wake up. There'll be just a renewal that'll happen in your spirit. That your spirit will become renewed and that you realize you need to be on fire for God. That it's time. This is the time. These are the end times, but this is the time for you to come on fire for God so that you are the ones who are winning the souls right now in Jesus' name.

We pray for that. I pray that in a decree right now, God, that You'll place that into their hearts, everybody who reads this, that God, You'll change their life, they'll wake up, and they'll finally realize, God, that Your glory is about ready to hit. They're either going to be left out or they're going to be a part of it. I pray, God, that everybody who reads this becomes a part of it. And Heavenly Father, if there's anybody out there who does not know You, does not respect You, and has not asked Jesus into their life, I pray right now, God, that they'll do that. And if you haven't, just repeat this after me: "Heavenly Father, I ask now that You forgive me of my sins. I know that Jesus died on the cross for me so that all my sins can be forgiven. I accept Jesus as my Lord and Savior, and I know that He came here for that purpose and that one purpose was to die for me. Thank You, Jesus. Thank You, God. And I change my whole life now in Jesus' name. Amen."

SHAUN: Amen. Thank you so much for that, Ivan.

REFLECTIONS ON IVAN TUTTLE'S EXPERIENCE

RANDY: Wow. Ivan met Satan. Thankfully not many can testify of that encounter! I appreciate how God used Ivan's experience in both Heaven and hell to contrast the dichotomy of being in God's Presence versus being steeped in the world and living apart from God.

God also gave Ivan a unique perspective on the world and the end times. God opened a window to creation as a portrayal of God's majesty and Almighty power. Can you imagine being given a front-row seat to the formation of the world? That Ivan was given this experience speaks to God's generosity in sharing His grandeur because God honors us that much to allow us to participate in His life.

What also impresses me is that Ivan was a believer before his afterlife encounter, but according to Ivan, only marginally so. Today he is on fire for Christ, having witnessed God's Love, and this contrasts to the lukewarmness that sadly represents the state of many in this world. I think Ivan's message after he died as a young man is prophetic—we need to get serious with God because there is no promise of a tomorrow.

SHAUN: Ivan is one of the few people Randy and I have talked to who had a significant hell experience. Like many of the men and women we've talked to, whether in hell or encountering demonic beings in that place in between heaven and hell, it was crying out to God or crying out to Jesus that made all the difference. In these circumstances, it is typical for either Jesus or angels to respond when a person cries out for divine help.

Similar to Jim Woodford, Ivan also had an encounter with lost children in heaven. I loved his beautiful articulation of what it looks like when mothers and fathers are at long last reunited with their lost children in heaven. Like we saw with Jim's story, this part of Ivan's story brought a strong reaction from people who have lost children long before it should have been their time.

Last, I have to call out what Ivan shared related to music in heaven. He gives one of the clearest articulations of how worship and praise through music literally shifts the atmosphere in both the natural and supernatural, exuding a heavenly power that is able to make demons flee. Don't underestimate the impact of getting your worship on.

FIND OUT MORE

If you'd like to encounter more of Ivan Tuttle's story, we encourage you to pick up a copy of his book *A Journey to Hell, Heaven, and Back* (It's Supernatural!, 2020). You can also connect with Ivan at IvanTuttle.com.

FIVE

CAPTAIN DALE BLACK DIED IN A PLANE CRASH, FIND OUT WHAT HE SAW IN HEAVEN

MEET CAPTAIN DALE BLACK

At age 19, Dale Black was the only survivor of an airplane crash. In the aftermath of that fatal crash, Dale suffered extensive life-threatening injuries and was taken into heaven where he received a deep revelation of God's love and God's ways.

Following the crash, it would take supernatural intervention from the Lord if he was ever going to walk again, use his left arm, or see out of his right eye. His dream of becoming an airline pilot now seemed impossible. As Dale's story unfolds, you'll see how God equipped Dale with the faith to overcome impossible obstacles again and again.

Dale would eventually realize his dream of becoming an airline pilot with a major U.S. carrier, logging over 17,800 hours of flight time.

Though Dale's story, you'll see how you too can partner with God to overcome the insurmountable hurdles in your life.

INTERVIEW WITH CAPTAIN DALE BLACK

RANDY: We call you Captain Dale Black because for 40 years, I believe, you were an airline pilot and you flew many missionary flights and you were also a flight instructor. And so I don't want to lead too much into your story, but you're doing ministry now with Dale Black Ministries and I have been an observer and a participant within that ministry as well. Dale, you have impressed me in terms of your story because of your love for the Lord. And I know that that evokes a certain degree of emotion. So if you can just walk us through what happened to you on that fateful day and how you were ushered into heaven, that would be greatly appreciated.

DALE: Yeah, no problem. Now I did spend 50 years as a pilot, much of that as an airline pilot with a couple of different airlines, but I trained pilots from just about every US airline that there is. And I ended up in my retirement as an FAA flight examiner in the Boeing 737, although I had flown 727s and 707s in the early days, I went up to the 747 and mostly Boeing equipment. In addition, my wife and I, we founded and owned a jet charter company. And most of our clients were Hollywood executives, Fortune 500 people.

That kind of led to when the body of Christ started bringing jet aircraft into their ministries. We did some selling of airplanes to ministries and we trained their pilots. In many cases we provided free services to a lot of ministries for a lot of years. But yeah, I always dreamed of someday retiring and becoming an author, just writing books and sharing the stories, the thousands of hands-on experiences that I believe God put into my heart and in my life, the trying to just not be a preacher. I wasn't a preacher. I wasn't a pastor. Wasn't a paid clergy at all. I was a pilot and I owned a business and we sold jet airplanes as a hobby. It became a wonderful thing to do. And God just led one step at a time.

It began when I was 19; I was a passenger. I was a volunteer co-pilot, but I ended up being a passenger on a twin-engine, propeller-driven aircraft called a Piper Navajo, a 10-passenger airplane. We were carrying cargo out of the Burbank airport, flying to multiples places around California. This was probably my 50th or 60th flight. I was pretty comfortable even though I was only 19. I had about a hundred hours in this aircraft, and I ended up becoming a volunteer co-pilot.

We arrived that morning. Three pilots were there. Gene was in the left seat. I was sitting co-pilot expecting to serve as a first officer, as usual. Chuck was in the temporary third seat behind us and we taxied out for takeoff. The weather was perfect. No rain, no clouds, great visibility—it was going to be another great July day. And this was July 18, 1969. The story was that Apollo 11 was en route to the moon. This is right in between their space flight between earth and the moon.

So we took off, and just before takeoff that day I got tapped on the shoulder by the boss, Chuck, who was my flight instructor. He was like my older brother in a lot of ways. And he told me to flip-flop seats. So I got out of the co-pilot seat. He got in and he strapped himself in. We started rolling down the runway—we're building up speed, 60 knots, 80 knots, 100 knots. We usually rotated the aircraft, which means you bring the nose of the airplane up. That's called rotation. And we usually rotate at about, oh, a hundred knots. And for some reason that day, I remember that Gene rotated a little early and surprised me. But the airplane went up. It started climbing up. The gear was selected up. The power was normal. And we had max thrust and the airplane started climbing normally.

Everything seemed pretty normal until we got to about a hundred feet AGL. We were just above the ground—AGL, "above the ground"—and I noticed then this strange sound, a horrendous whine and desynchronization between the two engines. Something was horribly wrong. That was clear within about a second. And I started scanning the dials to see what could possibly be wrong. And I was looking and about that time Chuck yelled in the cockpit—that's never done, by the way—he barked and yelled and said, "Let's land in that clear area over there," and he pointed with his left hand. I leaned up in that chair and I looked up and I saw what looked like a park, a bunch of green grass. And I thought, "Oh my gosh, we're going to be the headlines of tomorrow's newspaper."

CAPTAIN DALE BLACK DIED IN A PLANE CRASH, FIND OUT WHAT HE SAW IN HEAVEN

> *I thought, "Oh my gosh, we're going to be the headlines of tomorrow's newspaper."*

Strange, but that was my last thought. I watched Chuck grab the flight controls with both hands and turn them all the way left, all the way back against his chest. And that was my last memory. And the rest of it took place. I found out later, we had slammed into a building—my book says it was 70 feet tall, but on the 50th anniversary we had a ceremony there and the curator and the people who designed the building indicated it was 120 feet tall. That's quite a difference. But it doesn't matter how tall it was. It was a big building. And we impacted that at about the 75 foot mark at 135 miles an hour. And with that impact, the airplane just broke into a couple thousand pieces and there was no cockpit to be in anymore.

It's not like a big jet. This is a small airplane, maybe as big as your living room, but still that's not that big. And the three pilots, all three of us slammed into this immovable object, kind of like two cars going head on, on the freeway—that kind of impact. And it was lethal. It actually caused fatalities, of course, that impact, that blunt trauma. And then the three pilots fell, all three of us, just right next to each other on the ground. And the strangest part is right now. This is where I can tell you that I was looking down, confused, looking down at three pilots, not knowing that I was in that airplane—really not knowing anything was wrong. But in a sense I was scratching my head, looking down.

I looked at the first pilot in uniform and I go, "Man, he's dead, no doubt," but I didn't recognize right away who that was. And then I looked at the second pilot and, oh my gosh, that's Chuck Burns. He's my flight instructor. He's my good friend. And he looked dead. And then the third body was me. And I looked down—and I'm trying to say this quickly—but I had no pain, I had really no worry, but I was completely confused as to why I'm looking down at three pilots. One of those people was me, and it hit me all of a sudden, not about the cause of the crash, but what hit me was that I realized, "Oh my gosh, that's not me. I'm up here. That's not me. That's my body. I'm Dale Black. Not that my name means anything; it doesn't. That's just who I am. That's my name. And I'm Dale Black. And I'm up here. I am a spirit and I have a soul and I used to live in that body, but I'm not that body."

All of a sudden I realized in my youthful 19 years, I had always thought that I was my body. Maybe no one else has, but I sure have—I thought that was me and that maybe I have a spirit. I don't know what that means. And I have a soul. I don't know what that means. And I guess the soul lives forever, but at age 19 I had never understood this. And right then above my body, I realized I'm a spirit. I have a soul—my mind, my will, my emotions, my spirit, and my soul. They live forever. And that's who I am. And my body is nothing more than the tent. The thing that houses my spirit and my soul, but that's not really me. And I understood the eternal perspective. And I got that before anything else.

> *Right then above my body,*
> *I realized I'm a spirit.*

SHAUN: Dale, you were having profound spiritual revelations as you began your out-of-body experience. What happens next?

DALE: The next thing that happened was an ambulance showed up, and there's a good picture of this too in my book. It shows a picture of three Lockheed Aircraft employees who had run over. And these are engineers, so they know aviation and they know a little bit about fuel and combustion. And we had fueled drenched over everything. In fact, for months later, the skin on my body would peel off really thick because I was drenched in that same toxic fuel, but we had no fire, which was a miracle. I don't need to probably go into that. But it's a big thing to me that there was no fire. And there were two very hot engines that were sitting there amongst that fuel. And there was no fire.

> *We had no fire, which was a miracle.*
> *There were two very hot engines*
> *that were sitting there amongst that*
> *fuel. And there was no fire.*

Guys, you might want to know this. I was an NTSB volunteer. I was an FAA accident prevention counselor. I spent 50 years in aviation. That was my entire life. I did over a hundred accident investigations with big jets and small corporate jets and reciprocating engine aircraft as well. And almost every accident included fire. It's just so common to have fuel and heat and plenty of oxygen. And there was no reason logically in the world that our Navajo didn't explode, if not at the top of the monument, certainly down at the bottom of the monument. But there was no fire. I can only tribute God as a miracle working God.

Anyway, the ambulance showed up. There was life left in me. Thank God for this third paramedic who resuscitated me on the scene. I was put into an ambulance with Chuck—back in those days, that was common. We were thrown in the same ambulance, two paramedics working on us, and strangely my body was in there. I was looking through the window the whole time. I called it an ambulance chase. It makes no sense. You know, I love things that make sense. I love logic. I like business. I like math to a point. I like things that are quantifiable and that you can prove. Anything that you can't prove, I don't like. I'm not really the kind of person who talks like this. And yet here I am. God gave me this experience. And I guess it's like you, Randy, you have a similar kind of background in a lot of ways, I've learned. And here we are talking about what happened to us and it's real. It happened. And I can't explain very well how or why it happened.

SHAUN: You're not the first guest who has shared about chasing after their body while it's being transported in an ambulance.

DALE: Yeah? All I know is that my entire life changed in that moment when I woke up in the hospital. But anyway, back to the hospital. I was put on a gurney. Chuck was put on a gurney. I watched this from about five feet above my body. We were raced into the emergency room. Chuck went into one room, I lost track of him, and I went into another. And I was hovering above my body, just below the acoustical ceiling, watching them cut off my gray slacks, my white shirt with the epaulettes, and my wingtip shoes. A gray-headed doctor came in and started giving me the paddles. I guess I had been in and out of consciousness—life. I don't know if I was clinically dead. I would say I was clinically not dead. It doesn't matter. The point is I was right on the verge of life and death. I remember none of this in my brain. I remember every second of it in my heart. That's my spirit. And you are a spirit. That's your heart, and that's what God gave you. Okay? So make sure you understand what I had to learn the hard way—that you are a spirit and you have a soul and you live in this body temporarily. You live in this body temporarily.

I was in the hospital. I watched all of this. I think it's important that I share—if it's okay with you folks—that while I was looking down at my body, and I was still a little confused, I was not hurting at all, but I was thinking thoughts: "It's too bad. It's too bad. I'm only 19. Wow. I wish I had done more. I wish I could have lived longer, but okay. All right. I sort of deserve this." And then all of a sudden, a movie started playing in my mind, like a rewind of a certain part of my life. And I was 12 years old at a church camp in southern California called Cedar Crest. I had come down to an altar at a cabin and there was this athletic minister who had invited the kids, me being one of them, that if they wanted to receive Jesus Christ and you were honest and sincere, come forward and he would pray for us.

Well, I did, and he was praying for me. And I watched this event in my mind while looking down at my body in the emergency room, still July 18, 1969. And I realized that I had given my heart to the Lord Jesus Christ. I invited Him in. I meant it. I was serious. I was genuine and I had a zeal for Him afterward. And then I realized, wow, I gave my heart to the Lord when I was 12, and look at me now—full of myself, self-centered, self-absorbed, selfish to the maximum. I was friendly, but inside I was about as self-absorbed and self-centered as anybody ever could be. And I was ashamed and embarrassed and realized that I didn't deserve to live. I was a humongous disappointment to God as a Christian. Yet, for some reason, that's the only event that played in my mind—that one little section of my life. Of course, I had time to think about it.

Interesting—the most important decision, the most important act I ever did was back when I was 12. When I honestly, sincerely invited Jesus to take over the controls of my life. I guess that's kind of important because I'm alive now and I've survived over 50 years since that crash. I was born again, and God in His mercy answered the prayers of my grandparents who prayed for me daily by name. I think God actually spared my life in answer to their prayers. Not that I deserved anything, because I didn't.

Anyway, I started moving out of the hospital room backward, looking at my body and moving back, and I couldn't control it and I couldn't steer it. I didn't know what was happening. And it's written in my book. We worked hard at it with help from a couple of good editors, but we worked hard at trying to tell this story that's completely scientifically unproven—my whole story is.

> ***I started moving out of the hospital room backward, looking at my body and moving back, and I couldn't control it and I couldn't steer it.***

You can find out about the crash. That's everywhere. All the details are everywhere and they always have been. But actually what happened to me is—the best way to prove it is just to ask, "What have I done with my life since?" And I woke up four days later after having this experience in heaven and back. I woke up, and when my eyes opened on the morning of the fourth day in a coma, I was like a completely different person. Nothing looked the same. Nothing seemed the same. A ridiculous example might be, if you remember the movie *The Wizard of Oz*, you went from black and white and then all of a sudden it's color and dimensional—that's ridiculous. But in a way I felt like someone gave me new eyes when I woke up from the coma.

I tried to talk to the nurse and I couldn't. I was trying to talk and I had all these stitches in my face, and I felt like I was ripping my face apart. But I was trying to tell her—and I think the noise she could hear came out just muffled and garbled. But I was trying to say this: "Nurse, do you know God? Do you know Jesus, His Son? You've got to know Him. You got to know Him. He's real. Heaven is real." That's what I was trying to say.

And all she would say is, "Dale, are you awake? Doctor! Doctor! Dale?" And then they came in. I couldn't talk. All I wanted to do was tell them about God, tell them that heaven is real and that Jesus is the way to God. His Word is the framework. Everything we see around us, this is all just a test. This is basic boot camp, in a military training sense. This is a proving ground, a testing ground to get us ready for eternity with God in heaven. We have thousands of choices all day long. And what are we going to do with those choices?

So I came back completely changed—human, frail still, but my life has never been the same. I've never beat on the same drum. And I'm not trying to indicate that I've arrived and I'm some kind of a spiritual guru. That's not what I'm trying to say. What I'm trying to say is that all I want to do is please God. I'm human. I make mistakes. But all I want to do is please Him and do what He wants me to do and go where He wants me to go and say what He wants me to say when He wants me to say it.

Well, duh, I should have died on that airplane that day. My two friends did, and I go to their grave every year, especially Chuck's. And I think that every day that I've had is a gift from God, but here's the deal. When I feel like the love of God is not flowing through me on a regular basis, when I feel like there is some kind of a clog between God and me—that usually happens when I get busy, start thinking too much about the world that I live in. Maybe something happens. But if I get too wrapped up in this world, then those new eyes that I was trying to describe to you—when I was in the hospital on the fourth day, I felt like someone had given me brand new eyes. But when I start losing that spirit-filled anointing of God then I know exactly what I need to do.

I should have died on that airplane that day. My two friends did, and I go to their grave every year.

I've learned the solution to that problem for me is usually to grab my dog, a border collie, and put it in my car. And I go up into the mountains alone and fast. And I talk to God and I read His Word and I talk and I go without food. Usually the first meal, I can't fast right away because I've gotten too much in the flesh, so to speak. So I may have a first meal and then I'll have less and less finally no food. And by putting my body down, no food, the spirit inside becomes more dominant. When the spirit becomes dominant, then you have control over your soul and your flesh because your spirit is leading the way. And that's how God wants us to live as believers—to be dominant in the spirit, over our soul, even (our mind, our will, and our emotions), and certainly over our flesh, which is our body.

So that's how I have learned to live my life. And two weeks ago, what did I need to do? I needed to get to the mountains because so many things were happening and I needed to get away. And that's exactly what I did, except I had to put my dog to sleep after 15 years. This was my fourth border collie, so I've had border collies for a lot of years. I'm in between dogs right now, so I went alone this time and spent my time with the Lord. And I came back totally refreshed, totally happy, totally joyous. Because the spirit inside of me had gotten pushed down by the world and the pressures. And this world, is it not weirder now than it was a year and a half ago?

SHAUN: That's an understatement.

DALE: Yeah! This world is like, whatever was up is down and whatever used to be right is left and inside now—it's all mixed up, very confused. And what has happened? This is one way to say it, but the body of Christ has been compromised for a long, long time. And we, as the body of Christ, we are the only thing holding back the evil. Without us, evil overruns a lot like a garden. If you don't weed your garden, the weeds will overcome your plants and your crops or whatever. And we need to do the same thing with our world that we live in. We have to weed that garden and we, the body of Christ, we are the salt; we're the light. We're to take dominion. We're not to sit back; we're to take dominion over this earth. The world is satan's, but we are God's children. We are His army.

So anyway, that's part of what has changed me. A lot of people say, "Well, how do you know your story is true?" I can't prove it, but talk to anybody who knew me before. Talk to the people who know me now. I've changed. Everything's changed. I don't even take royalties. I don't care. We've given up what we had. We were relatively well-to-do and I grew up in a relatively well-to-do family and it doesn't matter. Money is just a tool. It's a tool to do God's will, His work. There's nothing wrong with working for the Lord. Even Jesus talks about that.

You know, what you guys have between the two of you is you have this love of the brethren. I just met you both for the first time, really, but I see the love of the brethren that is connected to your fiber. And that is more powerful than money or anything. The love of the brethren holds us together like cells in the body. And I love that about the two of you. And now I can be the third dude, possibly, because we we all three have that love. It's the love of God coming into us. When we are filled with His love, then it flows over to others. But we can't love others until we're full, because it's agape love, right? We have to have our own cup filled up, and then it's the overflow that allows us to be ministers of the love of God and the Word of God in this earth.

SHAUN: I think Dale just unofficially invited himself to be a third co-host for future episodes. I'm sure we'll be able to make that happen. Dale, I love that garden analogy and the weeds; I feel like that really captures the season that we've walked through and are continuing to walk out here in 2021.

I want to pull a little bit more on the thread of just the change from when you woke up. I was listening to your audiobook this weekend and like you just said, when you woke up it was like scales came off your eyes or you were looking through transformed eyes or different eyes. As your story unfolds, you just talk about how you actually cared about people. You had a burden—did they know the Lord? Had they encountered Jesus? You worried about their heart and where they were at. Just contrast that for us. How night-and day-different was that from where you were before the accident?

DALE: Well, I didn't want to make it sound like I wasn't a friendly guy. I think I was friendly. People in school thought of me basically as friendly. But I knew how to be friendly and still be selfish; that was easy to do. And what a person does in their spare time, free time, alone time—that tells a lot. And all I thought about was me and my goals and my ambitions. I had big goals in my head, big ambitions. And they were to outdo my peers, my brothers. I'm not trying to put anybody down. I just felt like I had been gifted and why not just maximize everything. And I wanted to travel the world and I wanted to own a lot of homes and apartment buildings. And I wanted very much to have—like the song when I was a kid—a girlfriend here and a girlfriend there. That just sounds horrible, but those were my thoughts.

My dad really helped force me to go to a Christian college. He said, "Just go for one quarter," which is like a semester, "and just see if you can get through one quarter." I was already enrolled in another college, which was going to help me with my aviation goals. But I went to this Christian college and I did like it, but I got kicked out of it for disciplinary reasons—not maybe what you think. I wasn't drinking and doing drugs, but boy did I want to challenge authority on that campus! I tried every practical joke there was. Some of it's funny; some of it's shameful. But I got kicked out of the college and I deserved it.

So when this airplane crash happened, I had been expelled permanently from a Christian college. I had shamed the family reputation in that regard. When I woke up, I was put in a wheelchair and the college actually heard that I had had this change. So it was set up and I rolled myself into the room and explained to the college authorities, and I gave my testimony and convinced them that I had changed. I would be an ambassador for the Lord Jesus. So they let me in, and it probably had nothing to do with the million-dollar check that we wrote them. No, I'm just joking, we didn't do that. They did let me back in. And it was a really good thing.

I stayed in that college and gained a lot of spiritual growth. That school is not far from where you are, Randy. It was in Pasadena at the time, but now it's called Point Loma Nazarene University. So that's where I got my degree. It was a great college. I'm really glad to have gone there. It was part of the change.

I stopped running around, stopped fooling around, started to say, "All right, what am I going to do with my life? Lord, what do You want me to do?" Strangely, there was no way I was going to be a pilot anymore. That was gone. And there was no way I was going to be an athlete anymore. I had a college athletic scholarship, and those two things were just gone because of all the injuries I'd had. And it just so happened I surrendered all of that. I believed that if I walked in the Lord's word, He would just give me whatever He wanted for me.

I was shocked and pleased that, little by little, I was able to get a baseball uniform back on. I couldn't use my left arm, but I never told my coach that. I just did what I could to try to get back to play baseball. I graduated and started flying and I learned how to compensate for all of the physical injuries I had. But I have to tell you guys, I had 20/200 vision in this eye and that was as good as it's going to get after a whole year. And then I learned that God's Word is true. The Bible says it. I mean, we're going to walk by faith, not by sight. And I was just a mess. My left eye was great, but my right eye had been cut in half. Both the retina and the pupil had been severed, and they tried to stitch it back together, but it was going to be difficult forever to become a pilot.

I learned how to compensate for all of the physical injuries I had.

In that day and age, it was much more difficult to become a pilot, but I learned how to exercise and speak the Word of God. Day in, day out, I exercised my eyes, ate for my eyes. About two years later, I took a really good eye test. You know how you exercise your arm, you build your biceps up? You can do that with your eyes. The simplest thing to do is go get glasses. But what I did was exercise my eyes and do the work of speaking God's Word into being. Anyway, I went 40 years with 20/20 vision in that injured eye, but I had to exercise and I had to keep speaking God's Word over that injury. My whole body is pretty much that same way. But I ended up getting most of my dreams that I had as a child fulfilled. But instead of grabbing those things like this, "Give me, God, give me," I do this (Dale raises his open hands).

RANDY: You know, Dale, I think we clearly understand the profound impact or change that happened to you through this experience. And since then, you became a very successful man in the worldly sense. Financially, you didn't have any reason to talk about your near-death experience or your afterlife experience. There wasn't any financial advantage to you. You told us that the royalties you don't keep and you dedicate it to the ministry. And we know that for anyone in ministry, it's not always lucrative. So the advantage is clearly to glorify the Lord.

You know, one of the things that is asked most about my experience is, "What was it like to experience heaven, the afterlife?" What are some of the more ethereal things in the encounter with the Lord that happened through that experience? Can you share a little bit about that? You know, because you had a very transformative experience after your accident and your near death.

DALE: I would love to. I seldom talk about the things that I want to talk about because people get lost. They don't understand it. I'm probably not a very good speaker to explain it very well.

I can write better than I can speak, I think, but I have to edit it several times in order to get it correct. But you know, everyone wants to know what I saw, what I heard—the eye candy and the ear candy. And that's great. I can do that. But what most people don't ask, but you just did, Randy, is, "What did you learn from your experience?" And what I learned is profound.

For example, when I got the near the wall around the city of gold, there was a welcoming committee that was just congregating there to meet me. It looked like they had been assigned to meet me at the exact time I was arriving. And this group came to meet me and greet me, and I could see their smiles and the brilliance in their eyes and what appeared to be love exuding from every pore of their being. They loved me. They absolutely loved me unconditionally. And I could feel it and sense it and know it, yet not one of these people was a blood relative on earth. Not one of these people was anyone I had known personally on earth.

That may frustrate a lot of people, because I've had a lot of emails come back and people have been relatively unkind about that. They said, "That's not possible. That's not right. Your story is not true because you're going to meet your family."

Okay, now, wait a minute, time out. You know, my family is on the inside. Listen to what God taught me, because maybe there's some value in learning what God taught me here. What do you mean they're not my blood family? They're more my blood family than anything else because we have the same blood flowing through our veins. It's the blood of Jesus that binds us together.

Even though I didn't know these people, they were my blood family. These were my brothers and my sisters in Christ. And nothing could possibly be more wonderful or more bonding than the blood of Jesus. So yes, they were my family. They *are* my family. And I would say this to anybody: If you know Jesus as your Savior, if you're on your way to heaven, you're going to love it. If for no other reason than you are going to be surrounded with the most loving people, your brothers and sisters, by the millions. They love you unconditionally for who you truly are. Not who you want them to think you are, but who you truly are. That was mind-boggling to me.

When I woke up in the hospital and I sat in my wheelchair, I thought about this a bit, and I sort of meditated on the event. I started realizing the Lord was talking to me: "Dale, did you notice any skin color differences in that family that I sent to you?"

And I thought, "Yes. Yeah, there would be what we'd call white and black and Asian."

"Dale, did you notice any gender differences there?"

"Well, yes I did."

"But did you notice it when you were there?"

"Absolutely not." And then silence.

I connected the dots in the silence, as God was talking to me, and I realized there is no racism in heaven. There's no racism in the body of Christ. There is no room for racism or gender identity. We are brothers and sisters and our bond is unbreakable. It's complete. It's thorough. It's fulfilling. This is what I learned in heaven—love is absolutely unconditional. And it's a hard to describe because it does not exist on the earth.

There's no racism room for in the body of Christ. We are brothers and sisters and our bond is unbreakable. This is what I learned in heaven— love is absolutely unconditional.

I go around always hoping for it, looking for it, praying for it again; it can happen. It could actually happen. I've seen little glimpses of that. You take a group of believers and you put them together and isolate them together. And they have one assignment. Your assignment is to do what Jesus told the disciples to do in the upper room—go and tarry. Basically, wait for the Lord. And so you pray and you fast—not every meal, necessarily—but you do some fasting and you read God's Word and you spend whatever time necessary. What happens is the walls of pride and ego and selfishness start slowly coming down. The masks start coming off. And what we find here is that the Holy Spirit's love, this unconditional love, gets more and more and more real in our everyday life.

You see, when Jesus told His disciples to go into the upper room, they became "in one accord." And when that occurred, the Holy Spirit came and descended on them. We can have that on this earth. We seldom have it. We seldom see it, but it is possible. I'll tell you, it's happened to me maybe a half a dozen times and I long for it and I love it. And this is what we as believers can expect, but we need to get rid of ourselves and let God have complete control of us. And then there's that oneness.

So that's just one thing. What did I learn? I learned that there is no racism. I learned that love is unconditional. And I learned that there's no sin. And it's kind of weird. We're all of us in rooms right now and we're breathing air and we don't even think about it. We're inhaling, exhaling. We don't think about it. Our minds are on other things. But when I was in heaven, I was trying to put my finger on, "What in the world is this? Oh my gosh, there's no sin." There's no sin. Can you imagine? I'm sure you noticed that yourself, but there's no sin. There's no jealousy. There's no pride. There's no selfishness. There's just nothing but the joy of God, the love of God, the life and the light of God that fills all of us and everything in heaven. That's the way God created it. We can have a glimpse of that here on the earth.

A lot of the people say, "Oh, Dale, I bet you just can't wait until you get to heaven. I'm sure you're ready to go right now, aren't you?" And on one side, yes. Sure. Of course. Yeah. But you know, all of us—you're already in eternity right now. You're already in eternity because you are a spirit. You are a soul. Those are going to live forever. Now the only question is, where will you go? But your body will die, unless the Lord returns. And He very well may in our lifetime. If we live to a normal lifespan, we may very well see the return of Jesus. And we can talk about that someday. But this is just the way it is. We have eternal life guaranteed, eternity guaranteed. In the meantime, the podcasts that you guys are doing, Shaun, Randy—you're touching lives. You're reaching people who would never be reached. And every day that you're doing this, every time you've touched someone, you're changing eternity for that person. So keep going, guys, keep doing the great work that you're doing.

For myself, I'm going to just keep doing the same thing on a small scale. I'm not a big-name ministry. Probably never will be, but I love God. And I want to have every breath matter for Him. And I want to help people find that Jesus really is the Son of God. He really was the Messiah; the promised Messiah was in Jesus. And you can trust Him. You can trust His Word. Follow Him with your life. You have nothing to lose and everything to gain. That's just one thing that I learned in heaven.

Jesus really is the Son of God. And you can trust Him. You can trust His Word. Follow Him with your life. You have nothing to lose and everything to gain.

SHAUN: Well, I think that definitely deserves an amen. And I have a question I want to ask you, but I want to give Randy an opportunity to comment. Obviously Dale is sharing things that probably relate to your stories as well. Anything you want to contrast or comment on with what Dale just shared?

RANDY: We are simpatico, Shaun. I've read his story. I know exactly what he means by the eye candy—people want to know about the color of the roads, the stone, the majesty of heaven, but it's all about the Lord. It's consumed by Jesus Christ. Everything that you speak about, Dale—I'm in a heaven reunion. You know, okay! Somebody gets me!

One of the things about your story in particular that has impressed me is you have a humility about you and an impact that is understated. I've got to tell our audience that Dale's impact in his ministry is profound, gargantuan, thousands upon thousands of people. But what's most important to you is glorifying your Lord. And I know that doesn't come naturally. It comes supernaturally through the power of the Holy Spirit. So you experienced meeting strangers in heaven who were of a familial nature by virtue of the blood of Jesus Christ. I had the same thing, you know, these are my brothers, my sisters. I had a similar salvation experience. My salvation experience was with a boy who prayed for me. See, this is another thing we have. We get emotional. How can you not?

DALE: Yeah shame on you, shame on you, Randy.

RANDY: I know, I'll repent after this. You know, you and I are methodical. I came from the medical side, you came from the aeronautics side. Both of them require a great deal of science and mathematics. And so maybe we don't naturally come from the bent of talking about the ethereal things. And then that profound experience.

The fact that there is no distinction of race, of gender, and any of these things that this world just emphasizes ad nauseam, right? It defines people in this world and people want others to be defined by that and in heaven there's none of that. So all of those things, Shaun, were certainly analogous to my experience. And I think that the takeaway that we will understand through this interview with Dale and others is that, if there's so many commonalities that we have, especially those of us who knew Christ going into this experience, there's something to this.

In a way, Dale, you're speaking to us prophetically. You know, this is what you, the reader, this is what you have to expect. This is your future. Do not fear death; do not fear dying. Heaven is in your future. I love what you said, Dale, that eternity is now. We're living in eternity. That's so special. And you highlighted that fact.

DALE: First of all, amen, Randy, amen to what you said. Praise the Lord for what you said and how you said it.

There are a lot of people who have said, "Well, I'm too old or I'm too sick or I'm too poor. I've been beat up so much. I've been abused. I've been on drugs." They have every excuse in the world to say, "There's nothing I can do. Nothing I can do here on this earth." And I keep thinking about how important was the prayer life that Jesus had when He was on earth. He would go away and be alone when the disciples were sleeping, and He would spend time. This is the Son of God. This is a guy with the Holy Spirit in Him, but He's on the earth now. He's in this fleshly body, but He's spending so much time with God in order to still have that oneness with God and to be able to have the power of God in his life.

So to people who say, "Well, I can't do anything. There's nothing that I can do." Well, there was one who was paralyzed. And of course we prayed for paralysis to be defeated. And that's a tough one. We know that's one of the more tough things to do. But this person finally understood that they could do something, even paralyzed. They could pray. They could spend their living days, every day, they could pray.

That is a purpose for a lot of you watching right now who say, "Well, I'm not a medical doctor. I'm not this or that. I'm not a successful business person." Whatever! Can you pray? Can you pray maybe a half an hour a day or an hour a day? If you'll pray an hour a day, you will change your world—if you'll spend an hour a day in prayer. And that's something to challenge everybody with. Find what God would have you do. Some have many talents, some have untapped reservoirs of talents and gifts. Turn those over to God. You want to have happiness and joy? There's nothing greater than taking what God's given you and giving it away.

You know, love is something you can't keep, something that must be given away. And when you give it away, you get it replenished on steroids. You just get more of it. So take what God has given you, give it away, and you'll find more joy, more peace, more purpose. That's what this living life is about.

And you know, I'm older than you guys by maybe six months, seven months, I don't know. But I really do think there's a good chance that we will see the Rapture in our lifetime if we live healthily as we should. And I'm watching this peace treaty, I'm watching for it to see if it's going to evolve into the prophetic treaty that will kick off the seventieth week of Daniel. Once that peace treaty is signed and confirmed—with the certain number of nations in a certain group of people, between Israel and certain people—then we can literally set our watch. How do I do that? Well, we can set our watch to the timetable that's in Daniel and then Revelation. And we pretty much know what's going to happen then. And it won't be the Rapture right away. There will be a Rapture and it will allow the body of Christ to not go through the Great Tribulation, but in my judgment there will be some seals poured out. I won't argue this with anybody, but I believe this is what the Bible says. There will be some difficulties and some persecution and this'll be required to purify the body of Christ. But since I opened my mouth and got started on this subject, I probably ought to finish and simply say, there is that remnant church that God has protection for—a supernatural protection during a time of difficulty all over the globe. God protects the faithful church. And there's scripture after scripture that I can allude to later. I'm working on a book on this subject, and so it's fresh on my mind.

SHAUN: I guess my comment would be that while every generation has thought they were in the end times, we definitely have seen myriad prophetic markers that we are in a unique time. There's a lot of things that seem to be lining up, so I couldn't agree more that we may be that generation. May we be so blessed, really, to be that generation that will see the return of our Lord and Savior.

I've got one last question I want to ask. And after Dale is finished with answering that, Randy, we'll let you lead us toward wrapping up, but I want to touch back on something you said earlier, Dale, about healing. You talked about how you were praying and contending and declaring for your eye, but that doesn't mean you were just sitting in a corner praying. You were exercising your eye and trying to read with your eye and doing a bunch of different things. So that was just one of many challenges that you had to overcome physically with the damage that had been done to your body.

Just talk to me briefly about that combination of contending, praying, speaking God's truth over the different parts of your body, but also taking action. I feel like often people just want to declare and pray, but I feel like actually taking action at the same time is a bigger faith step. By setting something in motion, you're partnering with what you're declaring, "This is going to move forward. I'm really believing that God is going to do that." I feel like that's where many of us stop short. So help us to just understand what you learned about that connection.

DALE: Excellent question, Shaun. And it's a complex question and we'll have to unravel it like an onion layer by layer, but yes, God is a healing God, no doubt about it. His Word is clear that He turned no one away. When Jesus was on the earth, anyone who came to Him for healing, He would answer the prayer and He did it in different ways. But He also said, "Your faith has made you well." So His Word is true—that healing is of God. No doubt about it. There's also no doubt that faith is an important ingredient.

Now, faith is not the same thing as hope. Hope is what most people in the body of Christ think is faith. It's not true. We need to have hope in the body of Christ. Hope is in the Bible, for sure. Hope is when there's something out there that you hope to get someday—that's hope, but faith is different. It's not the same. Faith sees that thing, grabs it, pulls it down into the here and now, and you possess it. That's the kind of faith that we're talking about in the Bible. The Bible says that faith comes by hearing and hearing by the Word of God. We get faith, which is the evidence that you can't see. But it is absolute evidence that you believe that what you don't see is here. So hope is out there, you hope to get it; faith, you grab it and you bring it into the here and now. And we need both. But faith is different.

Faith sees that thing, grabs it, pulls it down into the here and now, and you possess it.

When you pray in faith, things change. See prayer doesn't change God; prayer changes circumstances. If you pray with faith, then you'll change the world in which you live. So one layer is yes, we need to pray. We need to root our prayer in God's Word. If we do that, we're going to find that God's Word and His will are the same. God and His will, His Word and His will are not different. They are the same. And when we learn about God's Word in great detail, we find that God's will is always for healing. That's God's will—for healing.

There's another thing I've learned—we human beings, especially Christians, we want things to be simple. We want it to be easy and we'll take the simple route every time—the simple, easy, quick answer. And you know what? That usually doesn't work. For example, how many people do you know who have actually been cured of cancer? I mean really cured, not a five-year remission. I mean cured. How many people have you heard and seen who have been miraculously healed? The fact of the matter is, when you do research on the medical industry, we see that the Christian church is really not much different statistically than the world. If you're a Christian and you get cancer, the statistics show that that person is as likely to die as the non-believer. And that should not be the case at all, but it is the case. So something's wrong.

I have seen both sides of the spectrum for a lot of years. I have learned that when I was a young kid, I didn't even understand what I was doing right. It took me a while to realize that I had certain things in place that a lot of Christians don't have. I did not have in place—I didn't understand faith. I didn't understand healing. There was a lot I didn't understand, that God can and will do anything. But what I did know is that God works precept upon precept, and that God would bless my effort. I didn't understand how important that was because I grew up with an emphasis on effort. My dad and my grandfather, they were important in that respect. So I have learned that the way to get answers to prayer—especially in healing, but always—is to bring in the supernatural, with no limitations on it. To add the supernatural, miracle power of God to the natural. Put the practical and the natural together. When they work together, you can't lose. You just can't lose.

Take the most common, biggest healing problem in the world, cancer, which just happens to be an area of my expertise because I've spent 25 years in researching it. I'm not a medical doctor, so I'll let you know that. I have a PhD and I know how to research. And I learned that, thank God, God did this—not me. I just put the effort for it. But He taught me how to research. And there are others who are better than I am. But I learned how to research. And when my wife got cancer, I took my skill of researching aircraft crashes and I took those same skills and applied them over here. And I realized, my word, almost every one of us gives cancer to ourselves. If you've been diagnosed with cancer, it's not a disease that you just happen to get—oh, darn, it caught you. No, we give ourselves cancer by the way we think, by the way we speak, what we eat, drink, and how we handle stress.

So that's the natural part. But take the natural and learn how to speak right, think right, eat and drink right, and deal with stress correctly. Add that to faith in God, faith in His Word, knowing the power of God and how He always, always answers prayer. You put those two things together—that's where you can literally see mountains move. This is how I believe God created the universe.

I know this probably going beyond some people. It is certainly not you guys, but you know, we take a thermonuclear bomb and we have a little bit of plutonium in there. And we take this matter, and when we compress it, matter becomes just an enormous amount of energy. But if two times two is four and you take four and divide it by two, you come up with two—it's the same thing in reverse. You can take energy and turn it into matter. And particle accelerators accelerate photons almost to the speed of light, and they slam them into each other. I've watched and read and studied the effects of that impact of two photons colliding at over the speed of light, because they come at each other. What happens is this energy turns into matter. And so when God spoke, "Let there be light," He spoke it with faith in His heart and there was energy. There was so much energy because it's almighty God. It's faith in His heart, and it's spoken out of His mouth. Created matter, the heavens and the earth, and all that was created came this way.

We need to tap into the same principles that God did. It's important what we say. It's also important what we don't say. And if we're trying to get an eye healed, for example, if we're just trying to see, we don't want to say, "Lord, I believe that You're a healing God. Your Word says if I ask, I will receive. The door will open, and God You'll answer my prayer." And then as soon as I pray that prayer, I turn to my wife or my partner and I say, "Well, I just hope it works this time. Still can't see anything, not now. I'm no better." This is just an illustration. But it's the same thing with cancer. You can't talk that way in private and expect God not to hear you. Your spirit is going to hear what you're saying. You are—what does the Bible say? As a man thinketh in his heart, so is he. So what are you? Are you a man or a woman of faith? Or are you a man or woman of hope and no faith? Are you in the process of going from hope to faith?

One thing you want to do is you want to speak God's Word, which is His will. Don't let anything come out of your mouth other than that. And if you make a mistake, you do the same thing as you do if you slipped. If you're on drugs and now you've just gone back, you do the same thing. You go back to God and say, "Lord, help me. I'm so sorry. Forgive me for what I just said. I render those words null and void."

You want to speak God's Word, which is His will. Don't let anything come out of your mouth other than that.

Some people say, "Wait a minute, Dale, are you a name it and claim it type of person?" I don't know. I don't know what you call me. I don't know. All I know is this is how Jesus spoke. This is how the Word of God spoke. This is how we're supposed to speak and we're to take dominion over our own bodies, over our own world, we're to take dominion. Jesus said that if we will take dominion, we can walk on serpents and scorpions and we are not to fear. We will have power over all of the enemy, and nothing by any means will hurt us.

Anyway, back to your question, Shaun and Randy as well, faith is real. It's power. It comes out of your heart and then out of your mouth. And when it's real, when your heart and your mouth say the same thing, you've got faith, and that is going to move things. Blend the supernatural with the natural, the miraculous with the practical, and watch God work.

RANDY: Yeah, we've been to church. And we're so blessed by your sharing. You know, this is a man who has been to a place that doesn't require as much faith, if any at all. That is, when you're in heaven, everything is in Christ, as God has ordained, and you're there. So you don't need to hope or believe that there's a heaven because you know it because you're there. Dale is a man who's been there through a fatal flight accident and it is a wild story. So thank you so much, Dale, for sharing today. I know people have been blessed by your story, your message, and the fact that you are truly a changed man by the power of Jesus Christ. So we want to know how to find you and your ministry, your books—tell us how we can find you.

DALE: Well, that's very kind of you to ask. You can just go to DaleBlack.org and there we have an online church. You can find out we do videos, usually two per week. In our store, we have the books and we're trying to write about one book a year or maybe two books every three years. That's kind of our goal. And I've had an assignment just recently. I mean, I'm ready to do whatever God tells me to do. But recently I felt like He put His hand on my shoulder and said, "Okay, Dale. Good job. Well done. Good. Okay. A few little tweaks, but now, everything I've taught you, I want you to put it in writing."

And I said, "Lord, glad to do it, if that's what You're telling me to do. But if we're in the last seven years, what's the point?"

And, hand on the shoulder, "Dale, what did I just tell you? Put everything in writing."

"Okay. No problem." No questions asked. That's it. So now my thorough enjoyment is to try to write everything that He's taught me, and who knows what God will do with it. But that's my new assignment. But DaleBlack.org is where you can find us.

SHAUN: Well, Dale, let me also say thank you so much for sharing with us today. And you know, I've talked to Randy many times and got to meet you for the first time today. And I would feel like I was not getting the full experience if you weren't emotional. Because I feel like it just gives credibility to how much you've changed. You know, people often will say when they were in heaven, everything was love. How could you not be shifted after being immersed in love, after being that close to Jesus? So, I'm honored that you can just be yourself and share and be transparent.

That's really what we want to provide—a place where we can have conversations with people whom Randy and I find interesting, people whom we're excited about. But we also want to give you a place to experience real, raw, unfiltered answers. We may explore things that some people are going to think are strange. Some things might make you uncomfortable, but we really want you to encounter truth, transparency, and Jesus. I think we've definitely accomplished that in this conversation today.

REFLECTIONS ON CAPTAIN DALE BLACK'S EXPERIENCE

RANDY: From piloting cargo and passengers to piloting a message of hope to a lost world, that to me sums up Dale's transition after Heaven. Like many of our interviewees, Dale entered full-time ministry after his afterlife experience. I was introduced to Dale through a mutual friend of ours, John Burke. John told me that I had to meet Dale because we both cried whenever we shared our encounter with Jesus. Indeed, Dale and I became instant friends because we can empathize with each other.

What heartens me about Dale's story is the dichotomy of his experience. The memories of seeing those dead from his plane crash and his own grueling recovery after the crash are etched into his mind, and yet what he remembers foremost is the Glory of God in Heaven. I love how Dale speaks of people and places in Heaven as though they were his real home, which is absolutely true for all of us who profess Jesus Christ as our Lord.

Of course, one cannot escape the irony that God restored Dale's vision so that he could fulfill his dream of becoming a pilot and now, post the afterlife, God has given Dale a vision for sharing the great news of Jesus Christ throughout the world. Dale's transformation from a worldly perspective to a godly perspective is something we noticed in many of the stories shared, but in Dale's case, he literally flew from the physical realm to the spiritual realm and now takes people to an eternal destination. That tells how Jesus and Heaven will affect our lives.

SHAUN: Captain Dale Black was one of our early NDE interviews, so he'll always hold a near and dear place in my heart.

First, I want to note his prolonged out-of-body experience. Many people report being aware of their surroundings for a time before going to heaven, but Dale's spirit observed things at the crash site, in the ambulance as it rushed him to the hospital, and even what happened in the emergency room.

Second, I love how Dale's healing journey on the other side of heaven was an exercise in faith, declaration, and action. Not only did Dale pray and declare proper functioning over the broken parts of his body, he took action in the natural to realize those realities—notably doing regular exercises with his damaged eye—and was able to maintain 20/20 vision and pursue his dream of having a lifelong career as a pilot.

Last, I want to mention that when Dale came back from heaven, he had a burden for reaching the lost that he'd never had before. Even though his body was completely broken and shattered, when he first came out of his coma, he asked the nurse if she knew God. That same passion to tell people about Jesus still drives him all these decades later.

FIND OUT MORE

If you'd like to encounter more of Captain Dale Black's story, we encourage you to pick up a copy of his book, *Visiting Heaven: Heavenly Keys to a Life Without Limitations* (Destiny Image, 2022). You can also connect with Dale at DaleBlack.org.

AFTERWORD

WHAT DO THESE NEAR-DEATH EXPERIENCE STORIES MEAN FOR ME?

When we encounter these afterlife stories, it can be easy to get lost in the wonder of it all. The encounters with Jesus, angels, animals in heaven, etc.—it's all amazing. However, God isn't simply giving men and women these experiences to entertain us with a fascinating story. It's actually quite purposeful.

As I'm sure you're well aware, people are walking through some very dark days all across the globe. As we've alluded to earlier in this book, we've literally received thousands of comments and emails from men and women who had a life-changing encounter with Jesus as they watched and listened to our conversations about death and the afterlife.

Now more than ever, people are struggling with fear, depression, and hopelessness. No matter how much they might try to self-medicate to fill up the gaping holes in their life with entertainment, drugs, alcohol, food, or whatever other functional idol has been a coping mechanism throughout their life, it all falls short. The only true hope, healing, and life transformation is found in Jesus Christ.

These afterlife stories are a love letter that God has written to you. He longs for you to meet His resurrected son Jesus and to know beyond a shadow of a doubt that heaven isn't just some pie in the sky wish or hope. It's your future home. The place where you can spend eternity in His presence.

We hope that you've seen the numerous ways God has been calling out to you through these afterlife stories. We'll close with the prayer that Ivan shared at the end of his interview. It's your turn to respond to God; don't delay.

Heavenly Father, I ask now that You forgive me of my sins. I know that Jesus died on the cross for me so that all my sins can be forgiven. I accept Jesus as my Lord and Savior, and I know that He came here for a purpose and that one purpose was to die for me. Thank You, Jesus. Thank You, God. And I change my whole life now in Jesus' name. Amen.

ABOUT RANDY KAY

Randy Kay has founded four companies, including a biotech company and media company; served as an executive for Fortune 100 companies such as Johnson & Johnson; was the Corporate Operation Director for the fastest growing pharmaceutical company in the world; and he has served as chairman and board member for numerous nonprofit philanthropies and Christian ministries. He has written over 1,000 articles published in organizations such as the Wall Street Journal and Forbes. As an ordained minister, Kay is a sought-after Christian speaker and podcaster who can be found at randykay.org. He is also Chief Learning Officer of Pacesetters, a human development firm; CEO of TenorCorp, a strategic development firm; and Founder of Abundant Life, an online Christian personal development site.

Kay has trained and coached over one million people worldwide. His breakthrough research on thriving in life spans several decades, as he has uncovered practical ways to overcome trials. His near-death experience after Kay's heart stopped for thirty minutes gave him an exceptional insight into the afterlife with Jesus Christ. Kay has appeared on many television programs, podcasts, and blogs such as GodTV, Cornerstone Television, Charisma Media, K-Love radio, and NBC, reaching over 300 million people worldwide while sharing messages of encouragement. He lives in Carlsbad, California.

ABOUT SHAUN TABATT

Shaun Tabatt has worked in the Christian publishing industry for 10-plus years. He currently serves as a publishing executive at Destiny Image Publishers. Shaun is the host of The Shaun Tabatt Show podcast, co-host of the 2 Christian Dudes podcast with Randy Kay, and is the host of Engaging the Supernatural, which airs weekly on the PTL TV Network. Shaun and his wife Lynette are the proud parents of 10 amazing children.

Experience a personal revival!

Spirit-empowered content from today's top Christian authors delivered directly to your inbox.

Join today!
lovetoreadclub.com

Inspiring Articles
Powerful Video Teaching
Resources for Revival

Get all of this and so much more, e-mailed to you twice weekly!

LOVE TO READ CLUB
by **D DESTINY IMAGE**

Lightning Source UK Ltd.
Milton Keynes UK
UKHW021919110123
415177UK00021B/529